HOW FREE PEOPLE MOVE MOUNTAINS

Other Books by FRANK SCHAEFFER

Fiction

Baby Jack

The Calvin Becker Trilogy

Portofino

Zermatt

Saving Grandma

Nonfiction

Keeping Faith: A Father-Son Story About Love and the United States Marine Corps (coauthored with Sgt. John Schaeffer, USMC)

Faith of Our Sons: A Father's Wartime Diary

Voices from the Front: Letters Home from America's Military Family

Crazy for God: How I Grew Up as One of the Elect, Helped Found the Religious Right, and Lived to Take All (or Almost All) of It Back

Readers may e-mail Frank Schaeffer at FrankSchaeffer.com.

Also by KATHY ROTH-DOUQUET and FRANK SCHAEFFER

Nonfiction

AWOL: The Unexcused Absence of America's Upper Classes from Military Service, and How It Hurts Our Country

HOW FREE PEOPLE

MOVE MOUNTAINS

A Male Christian Conservative
and a Female Jewish Liberal
on a Quest for Common Purpose and Meaning

KATHY ROTH-DOUQUET and FRANK SCHAEFFER

COLLINS
An Imprint of HarperCollins*Publishers*

We'd like to thank our very supportive agent, Jennifer Lyons, and wonderful editor, Elisabeth Dyssegaard. Elisabeth gave a great amount of assistance in getting this book into shape. Also Kate Antony and Gretchen Crary of HarperCollins—we are lucky to have them on our team. Many friends and colleagues offered good advice—a few who went above and beyond were Genie Schaeffer, Julie Hirschfeld, Wendy Swart Grossman, Liz Stokvis, and Michael Duga.

HarperCollins books may be purchased for educational, business, or sales promotional use. For information, please write: Special Markets Department, HarperCollins Publishers, 10 East 53rd Street, New York, NY 10022.

FIRST EDITION

Designed by Kara Strubel

Library of Congress Cataloging-in-Publication Data is available upon request.

ISBN: 978-0-06-123352-4

08 09 10 11 12 ID/RRD 10 9 8 7 6 5 4 3 2 1

Frank's Dedication

*For my son Francis, a man of many talents who,
with top academic credentials (and virtually unlimited
opportunities), chose the vocation of teaching high school.
Through his devotion to his students and the sheer joy he brings
to teaching, Francis has changed countless lives for the better.
Francis gives me hope for our future.*

Kathy's Dedication

*For my father, Ed Roth, and my mother, Debbie Roth,
of blessed memory*

Contents

HOW FREE PEOPLE MOVE MOUNTAINS

1. Opposites Well Met

Kathy

Imagine Susan Sarandon and Clint Eastwood arm-wrestling. That's Frank Schaeffer and me. Frank helped launch the religious right; I wore the blue staff badge of Bill Clinton's West Wing. He's post-evangelicalism Christian; I'm what he calls post-Judaism Jewish. He's St. Paul and Fra Angelico; I'm sociology and political science. He's a sermon on Armageddon; I'm *I'm OK, You're OK*. A couple of decades ago we rallied on opposite sides of mass demonstrations. Once, we never would have met, let alone practically lived together for nearly a month.

I left two small children and a husband at home and Frank and I rolled down the tarmac together—highways, airports, rental car counters, hotels, restaurants. And though Frank was someone I had met just three times before, someone edgy, worldly, and handsome, this was no love affair. He was my coauthor. We were traveling to publicize *AWOL*, our first book.

We met the first time when I went to one of Frank's book signings. I showed up because he was a guy writing about a subject I wanted to write about. I went with the wild fantasy that we'd get to talking and this author whose work I'd read and admired would help me in some way. And then as I was leaving the signing, after we'd chatted, Frank wrote "Frank and Genie Schaeffer" and a phone number on a slip of paper.

I almost didn't call. I was out in the rocking world of politics a long time before I got married, so I looked at that number with a bit of a knowing eye. I figured that usually when successful men seem interested in your inner qualities, it's just a bit of a detour to your, shall we say, *outer* qualities.

"In the end, I called because you put Genie's name on the paper too," I confessed during a long drive to yet another book-signing venue after *AWOL* was published. "I thought you might be hitting on me."

He looked a little surprised, then parried, "That just goes to show you've been hanging out with your Democrat, Clinton friends too much. The whole world doesn't act that way, you know."

Ouch. Score one to Frank. Well, at least he was nice enough not to say I flattered myself.

Frank

It's hard working with Kathy. I sometimes feel like a patient in intensive care being visited by an overly cheerful friend. I have regrets. She doesn't. My favorite movie is *Blade Runner*. Kathy is more of a *It's a Wonderful Life* person.

Kathy sees things in material, secular terms: politics can change everything! I see things in moral terms: nothing essential changes, because we humans are sinful. Society is the way it is because of religion and philosophy, not because of resources, forms of government, or historical fluke. Kathy wants people to reengage in politics through referendums and direct participation. I think that good government works only if certain ideas are shared by enough people.

We agree too. Kathy and I both believe that something has to change—and change soon—about how we see ourselves, our country, and our world. We both admit that we could be wrong about a lot of things, and we know that our opposite upbringings have had a lot to do with what we believe today.

I was raised by Calvinist evangelical missionary parents to believe God is angry with us and always has been. He was pissed off with us from just about day one. In fact, He was so pissed off that He wrestled with making a choice between killing all of us in a flood or saving just one family—Noah's—so that later God could sacrifice His only Son to save everyone descended from the one family he *didn't* kill and/or send them to hell for eternity. God did this because Adam and Eve, not to mention Noah's great-great-grandchildren—that's you and me—wouldn't live up to God's pre-creation expectations. Cheerful, huh?

These days, faith and doubt are synonymous to me. But I still pray. Why would I bother to try to have a conversation with the angry God who brooded over my childhood? Because maybe He's not the terror concocted by Calvinistic theology: a peevish, blood-soaked, predestining omniscience.

I'm a jerk at times. Ask Kathy. Better yet, ask my long-suffering and lovely wife, Genie. But at my worst I couldn't see condemning my beloved grandchildren to hell for eternity just because they had a wrong idea about me or even if they said I didn't exist. If minimal compassion comes naturally to me, why? How could these feelings exist in a universe created by a nutcase vengeful God? Where would ordinary compassion come from? Are we supposed to believe that God is meaner than we are?

Sherlock Holmes said that if you eliminate all other options, then what remains must be the solution. Whatever all the stories in the Bible (and other religious traditions) mean and however they have been interpreted, what remains is love.

So, while I reject the fundamentalist religion that I was raised on, I'm still a religious believer, on good days anyway. That makes me the "God guy" herein. And like me (if the statistics on religious faith are accurate), most Americans look to God for help. So it doesn't make sense to leave God out of this book about what Kathy and I believe will give us a better future.

Of course Kathy and I are more complicated than our chosen roles herein. I have doubts, and Kathy turns out to be less secular than her lefty, secular, post-Judaism background might indicate. And then there is the playacting that all non-fiction writing entails: what writers *say* they think is really only a snapshot of a moving target. Writing is, by its very nature, an "act" of oversimplification.

Kathy

The second time I set eyes on Frank was Memorial Day week-end outside HarperCollins' midtown Manhattan skyscraper. Then the third time I saw him was in our editor's office when we delivered the finished *AWOL* manuscript, just after Labor Day.

So despite over a year of writing together, Frank and I barely knew each other. I had read what was in Frank's earlier books about him, he knew the outlines of my biography, and for a long time that was about it. We didn't chat.

I held back because Frank was a successful author while I was not even an embryo of a writer—more like a zygote—and knew I was lucky to have the chance to write a book at all. Better to keep your mouth closed and be thought a fool than open your mouth and remove all doubt. Plus, I was busy. My Marine officer husband, Greg, was deployed to Iraq. I was raising two kids, writing legal briefs, doing a bit of Democratic politics, and more or less keeping up with my wife-of-a-squadron-commander duties. Really, I had little time to spend on anything other than the task at hand. But probably behind my reserve was also the fact that Frank and I were from different worlds. Mine was secular, Ivy-educated, on the cusp of Gen-X.

We became writing partners on *AWOL* because we both were surprised to be "inducted" into the military family. Right or left, we both came from the kind of relatively privileged background where we assumed military service was not for people like us. As Frank said, "My son volunteered for the Marines but I was drafted." He meant drafted through his heart. I understood Frank's point. It was my husband who brought me into that world.

When we finally did spend some time together (other than via e-mail and on the phone while writing), Frank and I did a fair amount of arguing. But we laughed a lot too.

There were things we agreed on as well. We both buy into twin ideas: first, that life becomes meaningful and satisfying only when you contribute to something larger than yourself, and second, that our health as a country depends on our ability to engage with one another in a new and better way. What brings Frank and me together here is the belief that all the good things we have in America might just go away if all factions—red state and blue state, left and right, religious and secular—don't find a way to reengage with each other and with our country, our planet, and our future.

Frank

Kathy worked for the Clintons. She admires them. Enough said. But Kathy married a Marine. That gave me a reason to trust her when otherwise maybe I wouldn't have.

I warmed to Kathy when we met because she said she liked my books and she's smart, pretty, and kind. Now I like her because I discovered that she is also feisty *and* pioneer-woman brave.

Kathy and I first came together to talk about military service and how gratifying that service can be. And how the me-first society stands in the way of any kind of call for sacrifice. Where is a society headed that believes that the meaning of life (and the pursuit of happiness) is to buy stuff?

Kathy

"Ultimately, this is a question about God," Frank said. We were in a fabulous fish-and-chips restaurant in Pimlico, a neighborhood in central London, down a cobblestone walkway. It was six months after our book tour, and I was living in London with my family for the year. My husband, Greg, was on a military fellowship at the Royal College of Defense Studies. Frank was in town, and we were wrestling with this book, just starting to write.

"We either have a soul or have to believe we have a soul, otherwise what's the point?" said Frank. He splashed the malt vinegar on and took a bite. "Serving others is about the state of our souls—and the planet, by the way. We literally have to change to save ourselves physically, not just our souls. We're killing the earth, and all we can talk about is buying an iPhone!"

So that's Frank. Then here's me.

We're in our editor's office at HarperCollins. I'm pitching

this book: "Ultimately our culture today is a result of politics, the political decisions society makes." I'm pacing around as I say this, getting worked up over the point. "We became a society where what each of us thinks or wants trumps any idea of what we owe. We are a shopping society, an I-know-my-rights society, not by accident, or because it's part of human nature." See, I've been wrestling with why we all embrace consumerism—you are what you buy—and the even larger view that making personal choices is the route to freedom and happiness. If this way of orienting life not only harms society but even fails to make us happy, as lots of new books on happiness point out, then why do we do it?[1] "As it happens," I continue, "once upon a time around the 1930s we solved a bunch of social and economic problems by changing society in that way." (We'll get into this more later.)

I look at Elisabeth and Frank to see if this is working. Elisabeth nods. Frank looks noncommittal.

"We're not bad," I add. "We shape and are shaped by our society, and sometimes good choices have unintended consequences. An important take-away is that we once shaped our society to become like it is, and we can shape it again to change it."

"We can get there," says Frank. "If you and I can work together, then the whole country can."

"It takes more than that," I counter. "We're two people. We're talking three hundred million people here! *Major* change is hard, and we are so divided and cantankerous and aloof from leadership that we don't know how to work together. The question is how to get three hundred million free and divided people to move mountains."

2. Rock or Sand?

Frank

A few years ago I was in Las Vegas for a speaking engagement. As we were driving in bumper-to-bumper traffic up the glittering Strip that Friday night, the young man assigned to be my driver exclaimed, "I love living here!"

I figured it was a defensive statement, the kind New Yorkers with buyer's remorse make after they move to Florida then incessantly tell visitors how *great* the weather is. But as I glanced at his eyes reflected in the rearview mirror, he looked sincere and was grinning happily.

"You do?" I asked, trying to keep the incredulity out of my voice.

As far as I was concerned, Las Vegas was about as close to aesthetic hell as you could get outside of Donald Trump's apartment or some Saudi Arabian gold-plated palace.

"Yes, we have everything: Italy, Paris, New York—all of it. I never have to go anywhere!"

I looked at the throng of pale lumpen people milling disconsolately on the sidewalk. How far from the glamorized image projected by this benighted town were the actual people that I'd seen glued to the slots in the timeless twilight of my hotel lobby. I couldn't think of a reply. How on earth could this twenty-something driver have no idea that his Sheetrock-and-plywood "Venice" wasn't worth the crap it was built with, let alone mistake it for the jewel-like city that is slowly and tragically sinking into the Adriatic? And did he really think that his desert "New York" was what one sees on some crystal-clear morning from the walkway on the Brooklyn Bridge?

But my driver wasn't alone. He had swanky educated counterparts from coast to coast who had convinced themselves that living in "Tudor" mansions with Sub-Zero refrigerators or "Spanish castles" in Beverly Hills is living life to the fullest. The link between my driver and some rather more successful but no less deluded people—today's super-rich installing high-tech game rooms in their 20,000-square-foot "castles"—might be summed up as a twisted (and earth-destroying) preference for the faux rather than the real.

Rock or Sand?

Kathy

"America gets attacked, my son and a bunch of his mostly working-class buddies go to war, and President Bush asks the rest of America to go shopping!" Frank's voice rises, his face is red, and his eyebrows threaten. He scans the audience packing a large lecture hall at the Politics and Prose bookstore in Washington, D.C. "When one small group is asked to do all the heavy lifting and nothing is asked of the rest, something happens to the soul of the country." He stares hard at the well-dressed gathering, most of whom fall safely outside the asked-to-sacrifice group. He bites out his finish: "It may be legal, but is it right? What happens to a country that acts that way?"

Everyone gets stirred up when Frank speaks—he's like a revivalist, and there's a rush of people who want to respond. The book-related conversations Frank and I had with all kinds of people—young, old, conservative, liberal—would always broaden beyond the topic of military service. There was something else our audiences cared about: How do we get back to being the kind of society in which we all have a stake? How do we participate?

Frank had been talking about the sense of connection to other people and to our country that he got from being part of the extended family of the military—a connection he didn't get from his tony suburb or high-status career as a writer. He had just asked whether we can go on without a sense of connection to each other regardless of class, politics, or beliefs. This is what our listeners picked up on. Invariably our audiences would ask about how to find a sense of greater purpose in the jumble of modern life. What could be the new American dream?

We celebrate dreams, especially in America. They move us to action. Judging from magazine covers and television shows, Frank's right: many of our dreams have become consumerist dreams, boiling down to little more than to be rich, beautiful, and famous. And these collective dreams shape us because of our desire to fit in.

Frank

We Americans seemed to have developed a taste for crap on a gargantuan scale, replacing anything remotely transcendent, satisfying, or lasting. Jesus might have been thinking of the lifestyles we venerate these days when He spoke in the parable about the man who built his house on sand: "And the rain descended, and the floods came, and the winds blew, and beat upon that house; and it fell: and great was the fall of it."[2] Today we mistake sand for rock; worse, we don't even know what actual rock looks like.

Didn't Nietzsche talk about "everyday being oneself" and not belonging to "the herd"? But we *want* to belong. We *have* to belong! We can't change that. The desire to fit in is literally in our genes, an instinct bred into us more than a hundred thousand years ago in our ancestral home, where survival depended on acceptance by the group. So, if we can't change our desire to fit in, perhaps what we need to change is what it is we are fitting in *to*.

Rock or Sand?

Kathy

It's good to see the lifestyle we all seem to crave up close; it demystifies the glamour. When I was young I had jobs that put me around rich, beautiful, and famous people. I've worked in the White House, around billionaires in New York, with the entertainment industry. I even have a few friends who are rich and/or beautiful and/or famous.

In these envy-causing circles you see what today's new happiness research shows: there is very little correlation between material things and feeling good about your life.[3] It's great to be rich and beautiful *if* you also have people you love and work that matters to you. But in and of themselves, money and looks don't make a person feel satisfied about themselves or how they live. Flying first class without having anyone you care about or work that has meaning is just legroom.

A friend of mine is a billionaire's son who's not doing too badly himself. We were having coffee and catching up one day while he was in town for meetings, and he commented, "You know, whatever you have, whatever you can buy, there's always someone who has something nicer. There's always something else to want." His point was that there was no real end to collecting stuff. It was great to hear that from someone who has more money than I'll ever have. It reinforced that it's silly for any of us to get too distracted by wanting things.

Likewise, I've had friends explain to me why they have no

savings on a salary of $300,000 a year in Washington, D.C., or $700,000 a year in Manhattan. Lifestyles inflate; their cares haven't gone away.

Frank

Puritans, Quakers, Amish, Mormons, abstract impressionists. . . . Kathy and I aren't the first Americans to think about how survival is tied to the moral choices we make. The difference here is that we're not just talking about one group's claim to have found a "truth" that eludes everyone else. Instead we're exploring the possibility that there are truths that bind all of us together—if not always by choice, then by necessity.

We're back in the pitch session for this book at Harper-Collins. Kathy has just wrapped up another one of her sunny, no-fault assessments of our current crossroads. She actually used the phrase "We're okay" not as a joke but seriously, saying that whatever the problems in our country, no one is to blame.

"Kathy," I say, "*no one* is 'okay.' Okay?"

Kathy and Elisabeth exchange smiles. I know what they are thinking: *There he goes again!*

Elisabeth, our Danish editor, is kind, earnest, and secular. It's clear from her puzzled and patient expression that sometimes she thinks I'm from Mars. So how can Kathy, Elisabeth, and I reconcile our positions? We can't. But the message of this book is that this lack of reconciliation doesn't matter, because we have bigger fish to fry.

Rock or Sand?

Kathy and I are saying that we are being forced by circumstances to lay aside our pet peeves and save ourselves, even if we *don't* agree. What's the alternative?

Kathy

What is better than consumer dreams? I found part of the answer when I was lucky enough to really fall in love. I figured my husband would do the rational thing and leave his somewhat improbable job to make plenty o' money in the world of free enterprise. When we ended up not making *my* choice, I had it in the back of my mind that I could always come up with money myself. I was making good money when we married, after all.

But life intervened. The first few years of marriage took us to military bases in Japan and California, gave me two children, and found me back in law school. Suddenly a number of other things seemed more attractive than a largish salary. When I graduated from law school, I had choices to make. Would I go back to work or not? Would I put on a suit and leave the house for the entire day, send my kids to day care or leave them with a nanny, and lose the free time I loved and the feeling of the sun on my bare arms in the afternoon?

To put it another way, would I more than double my household income? It would let us move out of our townhouse— which, frankly, I was a bit embarrassed to invite some of my fancy friends to—and into something a bit more elegant. I could send my children to private schools. We could vacation in Italy instead of at the local beach. We could move up that ladder.

But by that point, I'd gone up and down the income scale by choice a couple of times. I was aware that there is a well-known process—it's called the "hedonic treadmill" by psychologists—in which you get used to having a certain amount of money, so what you have in the way of material goods fails to satisfy or give much of a thrill once you've adjusted to it. When you haven't gotten your hair and nails done in six months, indulging in a salon visit is a pleasure. When you get your hair and nails done every Monday, it's not much different from brushing your teeth.

I was living my own little small-scale version of what the scientists studying happiness were concluding on a grand scale: that stuff we once dreamed would satisfy us turns out to be just the next thing that gets old. So consumer dreams have their limit. And self-expression, the idealistic twin of consumerism, also has its limits.

These two things—stuff and self-expression—are the closest things we have today to a national religion. As a nation, our past dreams have included Manifest Destiny and the desire to be a beacon of freedom, a melting pot, the shining city on a hill. Why talk about consumerism when we're writing about finding a joint purpose? Because consumerism has become the anti-dream, the thing that distracts and pulls us apart, just when we need to come together. Our dream today is about things that don't satisfy.

Frank

This is the second time I've been part of a project that addresses the so-called big issues. I hope that this time I'll tell fewer lies. The first time involved sell-out crowds as I tagged along with my late father, Francis Schaeffer, and actually became his sidekick (for a few years) on the big-time American evangelical circuit. I was zealous and sincere, at least for a while.

Dad and I were instigators of the beginning of the religious right. Our "issue" was abortion. That was back in the 1970s and early 1980s. By the time Dad died in 1984, he was known as a founding father of the religious right, and I was disillusioned and on my way out of the evangelical subculture our family had become "royalty" in.

In the bad old days I wasn't lying on purpose, but when you are a zealous anything—evangelical, Marxist, feminist, capitalist, Democrat, Republican, whatever—you express your zeal by lying. The lie is always the same: you're *absolutely right* and others are *absolutely wrong*. This is a lie because nothing is as simple as any zealot, of any persuasion, thinks it is.

I've quit believing in ideological, let alone theological, purity. We guess. We hope. We muddle along. But there are no theological ideas worth hating anyone over.

Today I describe myself as a Christian who attends a Greek Orthodox church, a believer who has enough doubts to qualify as an agnostic on some days. In other words, to borrow the biblical adage, I "walk by faith, not by sight."

Nevertheless, I regard my evangelical friends as essential to the well-being of our country, and not just because there are lots of them. I have a deep appreciation for the often underestimated contribution to our national life that the evangelical community makes. Shorthand: if there were no evangelicals (and many other devout people), there would be fewer hospitals, missions to the poor, women's rights, and civil rights. It would be a far crueler world without the contributions of the myriad of people who have tried to live by the light of Christ.

Kathy

When people's convictions—their efforts to live by the light of Christ, as Frank says—lead to good action, then the convictions are great. But I care ultimately more about good actions themselves than the source of inspiration. Why? Because we need good action whether the source is the Talmud, Buddha, the Koran, or secular humanism. We cannot and will not all be Christians. But we can all be people of compassion and action. And we should remember at the same time as we applaud belief that belief separate from action can be a kind of consumerism—our point of view can be just one more thing we're attached to because we own it.

3. Things That Change, Things That Endure

★ ══════════════════

Kathy

Life in London, like any expat life, brings into sharper focus how America is both different from and the same as other countries. During the year Frank and I wrote this book, my husband was on a course that brings together colonels and generals from around the world, forty-four different countries in all, to talk about international politics and diplomacy, learning to prevent rather than conduct war.

In many ways the course is social as much as anything else; its point is to build ties between people, and perhaps understanding. Chinese and American, Indian and Pakistani, first world, third, and Middle East play racquetball and drink their respective beers and orange juice between seminars, becoming friends.

At any rate, it was a social year. We got together for dinner parties and the like, and often ended up talking about the day's lecture topics. On one occasion, the conversation around the dinner table was about an item on the syllabus, national identity. "What does it mean to be British?" mulled a Royal Navy captain. "A lot of people ask that question these days. It's not clear when the most popular name in the country is Mohammed." "It's hard to say what it means to be French," said Luc, a colonel in the French army.

These are knotty questions for countries that have been built on a certain ethnic and historical identity. For centuries their national characteristics have been tied to a specific heritage, religion, and ancestors. When these countries open up to immigrants—when they are not merely a set of people who've been sovereign on a plot of land over time—then what are they?

For our friend Noh, from Japan, the question was uncomfortable, practically in the realm of taboo. Their inheritance from World War II has left the Japanese averse to anything that smells like nationalism, as the question of national identity seems to do. "We would never talk about this in Japan!" he said, his hands up as though pushing away spoiled food.

But America is a different kind of country. We ask the question what it means to be American because from the beginning we were built on an idea. We've always had to find some other bond besides shared family trees or land to bind us together.

The ideas that lasted, that rang true for us through the generations, were the ideas in our founding documents, ideas of freedom and opportunity. But what freedom meant, what opportunity meant, what they required of us and how that combined with the purpose of America itself—that has changed over time.

Frank

We don't talk about the British dream, or the Moroccan dream, or the Korean dream, but somehow the idea of the American dream has made a sort of sense. It still does, or could anyway.

Red or blue, we're all in the same boat. That "boat" is our common dilemma: how can you figure anything out when you are part of the equation you are trying to decipher? So let's admit we have a basic problem when it comes to self-evaluation. The dilemma was best articulated by Darwin: "Can the mind of man, which has, as I fully believe, been developed from a mind as low as that possessed by the lowest animal, be trusted when it draws such grand conclusions?"[4]

Probably not. Some religions came up with a similar "Darwinian" insight pre-Darwin: the recurring idea that there is something wrong with us humans, a sort of original sin, a state of fallenness and depravity that, for instance, Protestant reformers including John Calvin believed in. Calvin said that sin rendered human thinking a useless conceit. Some evolutionary psychology goes a step further, saying that evolution's design actually builds in self-delusion as the primary means to get humans to pass on our genes. We are deceived into wanting to propagate, survive, and prosper, not so that we can be happy—something evolution never had in "mind"—but so that our gene pool may go forward. Since this kind of self-delusion operates on a subconscious level, we don't even know we are machines, and so we keep droning on about free will, meaning, love, art, God, and so forth. In that sense nothing we do is our fault, and nothing is a real achievement either. We are manipulated victims.

I don't believe that is true, but let's say, just for a moment, that the grimmest of both sides of the debate—the religious determinist's and the Darwinian determinist's ideas of perpetual victimhood—are correct and we're all slaves of sin, genes, or both, or at any rate so caught in the machine we live in that we can never know anything objectively. Now what?

Since we are delusional, then of course knowing this is just a further delusion. Do we give up? For instance, do we stand back and watch our earth become uninhabitable just because we're stymied when it comes to fully understanding ourselves?

Some people seem to be advocating a sort of giving up. Princeton University professor and molecular biologist Lee M. Silver writes that life has no final meaning: "Although I keep listening, because it's depressing not to, I have yet to hear a good answer, other than there is no point."[5]

But if everything is really that hopeless, why do we long

for meaning? Where does the urge to look for truth (or truths), large or small, come from? And what is the best expression of that longing, and of the inner knowledge most of us have—a few depressed molecular biologists and theologians excepted—that in fact our lives and our place in the universe *do* mean something, even if that something is hard to pin down?

Kathy

Our country had a purpose at its founding and that national purpose was twinned with a purpose, a dream, for its people. As long as there has been an America, there's been an American dream of a sort, though that phrase wasn't coined until the 1930s. My grandparents immigrated a decade or more before the term was first used, but I think they would have understood the idea immediately.

My father's grandfather fled the crumbling Austro-Hungarian empire, fled the pawn-like position of having to alter the language he spoke as wars and treaties redrew the boundaries. Though it cost him all the money and social standing he had acquired as a prominent rabbi, he moved his whole family, all ten of his children. My grandmother was the second oldest of those children. She'd gone to school in the old country—because her father was both influential and sympathetic to his smart daughters, she and her older sister received a special dispensation to attend high school (there called gymnasium), which otherwise was only for boys. They sat behind a screen, taking notes, unable to see scientific demonstrations, unable even to ask questions. College was out of the question. Her younger sisters and brother came to America young enough to go to school here, and they all went to college. My grandmother married, raised children, and stayed committed to her orthodox upbringing. And in the 1960s, when she was sixty-four, she got her B.A., in math.

The middle period of the twentieth century was one of many times that the American dream was connected to an idea of American purpose. My grandmother's successes were America's successes. When her family was welcome here, thrived here, and contributed to their new society, it was a rebuke to Nazism. When my father left the one-bedroom apartment that housed his family of four while he was growing up and worked his way through medical school, it was a triumph not only for him but also for America, which through its acceptance of outsiders and the mobility of its people, proved itself better than the Old Country or the Soviets. As the immigrant says: what a wonderful country! And this sense, one's personal good is also society's good, gives a person a robust sense of well-being. It was the sense the pioneers had, the sense the civil rights activists had. And it's something we lack today.

Frank

I think many of us share an innate awareness that we're not alone. I don't know what other people mean by the word *prayer*, for the same reason that I don't know what they really mean when they say something is green or yellow. I see with my eyes, not theirs.

To me prayer means that I feel God's presence. Love and communication seem to go hand in hand. For instance, I'm happy when my grandson, Benjamin, or my granddaughter, Amanda, calls and we talk. At those times I know the truth of who I am better than at any other time: a fifty-five-year-old man worrying over his eleven-year-old grandson's new drum teacher and his fourteen-year-old granddaughter's boyfriend, as deeply involved in their "small" dramas as in anything "important" going on in my life. I like hearing from them. I assume our Father in heaven likes hearing from me.

In any case, as I walk down my moonlit drive on some crisp winter day and everything strikes me as beautiful, it seems natural to tell someone how I feel. And when Genie told me she had a lump in her breast, it seemed natural to ask for help. When it turned out to be nothing, "thank you" seemed to be a natural response. When my son John was deployed to a far-off war, who was there to talk to other than God?

Kathy

The mega-blockbuster book *The Purpose Driven Life* has an answer about what our purpose should be—it's about Jesus as a personal purpose. This book has sold more copies than any other hardcover in America's history—twenty-five million at last count. But I'm a political person, so I tend to see things through a less supernatural lens. In my role herein as the "secular guy" (as Frank would say), I see that purpose has something to do with how and why we order ourselves in the society and times we live in.

In our country we have had a sense of shared purpose at certain periods and not in others. When the American dream, a shaper of personal purpose, works in concert with the great national purposes, that seems to be when we are most in sync, when individuals and the country thrive and are at their best.[6] That was the case during and just after World War II, and it seems to be what people remember with such fondness about that time. It was the case in an earlier era too.

In our first century as a country the dream was about a new kind of freedom for America's citizens—albeit white men—self-sufficiency, or the freedom that meant no one controlled your livelihood, your land, your destiny. You had no local lord or sovereign but yourself. That freedom required something, though: doing the work of the local lord or sovereign, being part of running the larger show. The practical side of the dream involved the possibility of owning your own farm, small trade, or shop. It was a dream of opportunity: no matter how poor you were, if you worked hard, you would be able to attain this dream. This promise put Americans on equal footing. And the concept of equal footing has been a source of our unity as Americans throughout history, even through today.

Things That Change, Things That Endure

Each individual who cleared land for a farm, built a shop, or developed a trade expanded the country. Likewise, the expansion of the country provided for the continual nurturing of the distinctly American dream of the freedom and opportunity to become self-sufficient. As sixth graders know (or at least used to know), this was America's idea of purpose, its Manifest Destiny. Individual dreams and national purpose worked in synchronicity: self-sufficiency and expansion.

The era of equal footing and self-sufficiency of the small, independent owner and producer died with industrialization in the late nineteenth century. We had a long period of turmoil when the conflict between capital and labor—owners and workers—threatened to undo the very basis of what our country stood for: the equal and independent status of all men. We emerged from it at last, into the modern industrial era of the twentieth century, with a new dream: freedom and opportunity were redefined and reenshrined as the new American purpose. Gone was the old cornerstone ideal that we could all achieve self-sufficiency. But after a great deal of pain we'd found new grounds for equal footing among citizens by redefining Americans as consumers. After all, if we were not all owners or producers anymore, we could all be consumers. This was not something that just happened; this was a conscious, debated, and at long-last, settled course of action.

Our perception of freedoms and opportunities therefore became more and more consumerist. The American dream of this new era of early modernism, the 1930s through the 1950s, was of a house and a car, a chicken in the pot, a job with a pension—security and comfort in exchange for working hard and playing by the rules.

It worked because national purpose and personal purpose were in sync once again. Someone who lived the American dream of making money or buying a car could feel patriotic—demonstrating the possibilities of the American kind of freedom, compared to the individual-crushing systems of communism or fascism. And in the first generation of consumerist purpose, the 1930s through the 1950s, our system lifted most of the people in the country from poverty—it seemed demonstrably good. People could also feel patriotic by settling new territory in the expansion of distinctly American ideals—in the civil rights struggle, for instance. This was my family's experience when they became middle-class and belonged (even as a minority) in a way they'd never imagined in the old country.

We are now at a point late in this second era of our history, and we've become more disconnected from national purpose. The struggle with communism is past, and what were once distinctly American ideas of individual rights and freedom have gained currency in the rest of the developed world. Those are victories. Less good is the fact that our individualism has now trumped the stake we once had in steering the country. We Americans aren't members of civic groups anymore; we've delegated our public interest (most people write checks rather than attend meetings).[7] The reinvented American dream, unmoored from a larger purpose, just became more of the same: upward mobility, more self-expression, more stuff—bigger houses, more cars, more TVs.

My point here is that the American dream and American purpose aren't static. And they don't change on their own; *we change them*. There's good evidence that it's time for another reinvention.

4. God, Secularism, and a New Agora

⭐ ═══════════════════════

Frank

Some things change, some things stay the same. The value of the authentic over the fake, for instance, is something that is eternal. The fate of the authentic Venice tells a story about our society. The real is allowed to crumble while the world beats a path to a fake. So which Venice do we want to live in? What is authentic?

Many years before my father became a famous religious leader, he took me to the Metropolitan Museum of Art. I was seven and in a wheelchair, having just had my left leg operated on to correct some of the disabling effects of the polio I caught when I was two. In the summer of 1959 we were staying with friends on Long Island so that I could recuperate before returning with my parents to their mission in Switzerland. I told Dad that I'd much rather visit the zoo.

"Art is important," he answered.

I'm grateful Dad didn't listen to me. He showed me a Vermeer instead. I liked it, though I didn't like the squeaking of my wheelchair's rubber tires on the oak parquet floors of the upper galleries. It made people glance at the little boy wearing a hip cast. I was tired of attention, questions, and sympathy. And the hush in the galleries reminded me of my least favorite place: church.

To me church was sitting still in our chalet living room/chapel while my dad's voice rose to a higher and higher pitch of intensity until he was shouting phrases I knew so well that even by age six or seven I could have completed almost every other sentence for him: "The finished work of Christ on the cross!" "A personal Savior!" "Took our sins upon Himself!" And these yelled "certainties" were in stark contrast to the humane way my father approached art, faith, and life when not making a point in public, maybe something like the difference between a politician's stump speech and the more nuanced conversations he has with his family.

After Dad squatted down to see what the painting looked like from where I was sitting in my wheelchair, he said, "It has a glare on it from down here." That's when he lifted me so I could get a better look. He helped me balance on my good leg while I stood.

"Look, really look," Dad said.

My father has been dead for almost twenty-five years, and

it's almost fifty years since he first showed me "Young Woman with a Water Pitcher." She's still standing by her window bathed in the gentle, translucent, indirect daylight that every good figurative painter since (and cameraman) has been inspired by. And, judging by her demure inward-looking expression, her thoughts are as peaceful as ever. When I visit her I sometimes still hear Dad talking about how Vermeer made the simplest of life's moments sublime.

"It's ordinary things in life that matter most," Dad said. "He painted for us, not the elites."

But elites aren't always bad. Sometimes they choose to do something better than commission ego-stroking paintings from the likes of Rubens, build a fake Venice, rape the earth, or drive an SUV. They also have the money to preserve our memories. And in those memories we sometimes find hope and even spiritual truths that can guide us into a better future.

It's lucky for America that there were no income taxes in the nineteenth century and that there were Americans with money and Europeans with art. In the late 1800s, railroad financier Henry G. Marquand collected then gave the Met many paintings and was the museum's president for a few years. His gifts included "Dad's" and "my" Vermeer. In 1892, in the magazine *The Collector*, one editorial writer said that Marquand was "one of the men among us who have looked beyond the present." He was "the greatest collector in America, because he [collected] not for himself alone, but for a whole people and for all the world."

It is that mystical spirit of transcendence—Marquand's

desire for beauty, expressed by doing something for the world and not just for himself—that Kathy and I are reaching for here. When Kathy pushes her sweep-of-history view on me, I get what she's saying about how things change. But there are also some things that endure. And it is with those changeless things that we need to reconnect.

Kathy

I rub my hands, because it's cold in my temporary London flat, where I'm stirring soup for dinner while talking to Frank on the phone. "You know, Kathy," Frank is saying, "your problem is that you talk about shared purpose as though it's a great accessory, something you can just pick. For you it's not urgent, it's not a calling. You make it sound as if America should just sit down cross-legged in a circle and use some kind of feminist kumbaya decision making to come up with a purpose that's not too offensive to anyone. Where's the thunder? Where's the burning bush?"

"Well, that's just the point, isn't it?" I say. "One man's burning bush is another man's hallucination. I mean, who gets to decide what's real and what isn't?"

"Oh, puh-lease." Can you hear someone roll their eyes? "Now you sound like the same relativist dead-enders I thought we're criticizing here. If nothing's real, we still have to act as though it were or else commit mass suicide. And this, by the way, is where religion has an edge: it says the bush is real." Before I can answer he goes on, "And the bush is burning, but not with God—with carbon poisoning. This is literally fate-of-the-world, don't-change-anything-and-we-die material here. Right?"

Frank loves the apocalypse; he feels at home in it. For him, the looming environmental disaster is why we need to pull together. And I agree, despite my occasional squeamishness about his drama. I buy it. If ever we needed to work together to solve something, it's now, as our planet is being trashed. But it's not enough. Just because the path we're on may be deadly, incanting that fact isn't enough to enable us to change it. And even if by some miracle, some fabulous technological breakthrough, we are able to avert the most pressing environmental disaster, the next one will be hot on its heels, because we have a more fundamental problem.

"We've got an enormous task in front of us," I say. "The world has become small enough that the big issues press against us no matter where we live—environment, poverty, war. But we're not going to move the mountain by talking about how important it is to move it. We're going to move it after we figure out how."

"We'll get there with God's help! *Praise Jesus!*" Frank says, imitating a TV preacher's voice. Now he's teasing me.

"There's too many of us," I answer, doggedly on message. "How we move this mountain is a new problem. In the old days, the king, emperor, pharaoh, or pope—whoever decided the big projects—basically ordered people to move the mountain, if it came to that, and they obeyed. Presidents were more unquestioningly followed in the past. Now we're in a different stage. We're free and cynical. *We* have to figure out how to pull off dealing with each other. Even the most inspirational leader in the world won't be enough, without us rolling up our sleeves, too."

"What are you talking about?" Frank asks.

"We have to find a way to decide together that the bush is real, without either God or Caesar telling us to believe that. We have to find a way to act together. So I think our purpose now is to learn how to live together, decide together, act together: Unlike the title of your dad's book, the question is not 'How should we then live?' It's 'How should we then live *together*?' How can we best interact, share information, make decisions together? How do we link ourselves up with each other? We need a new agora!"

"Agora. That's very blue-state, isn't it?" Frank laughs.

"All right. But I think that says it. The agora was the place in ancient Greece where people got together, talked about the things that concerned all of them, decided together how to act. It's what made early democracy possible. We need to all learn the tools, the tricks of the agora, if we're going to be able to engage with each other and to somehow *do* global projects while still being free people. But we need something that hasn't yet been invented—a turbo-agora, agora 2.0—to take us beyond the several hundred togas of the Greek agora to the several hundred million of our interconnected country."

"You want everyone to be a senator?" Frank doesn't sound convinced.

Frank

We are a long way from Kathy's "new agora." Kathy talks about needing to make a connection to one another. She sees this as some sort of political connection, an outgrowth of policy. But let's start with the personal. How can you build consensus with people who are preoccupied with the next shiny thing they can buy? The answer is that you can't.

So maybe we need to remind everyone that "moving up the ladder" is not enough in and of itself, as a life purpose. It needs to be coupled with contribution—to family, community, even to nation. With all our success and money in America (relative to what people used to have, relative to the rest of the world), we're not happy. Maybe it's time to literally look at ourselves in the mirror. Those frozen-by-Botox masks more and more of us wear are a grotesque visual warning about where the "values" of American consumerism, materialism, and greed are taking us and also where they are preventing us from going.

How did we get here? We have elevated "I want" to a national obsession. We've made a soul-destroying and earth-destroying choice. Loving stuff for stuff's sake has failed.

Kathy

When I was in my early thirties my dad moved out of a house he'd been living in, and I came over to clear out some boxes

I had stored there. In one box were some journals I had kept haphazardly over the years, starting from when I was a teenager. There wasn't much to look through; mostly I wrote only when in the grip of unusual angst or boredom. But I noticed that the same themes kept coming up at ages eleven, fifteen, nineteen, twenty-four, and so forth. Each time it was as if I were thinking about the matter afresh, and it made me realize that most of us have themes that probably resonate for us our whole lives. For me, one of those themes was one of the questions Frank and I debate: What's your source of authority? What's the best basis on which to make decisions that matter?

The roots of that question for me probably began long before I asked questions. Unlike Frank, who was raised as one of God's elect, I was raised not to believe at all. I picked up the idea that there is no God at a Passover Seder, standing before my grandmother's lace-spread table in the glow of candlelight reflected on silver, when I was five years old. I was mulling the words of the Haggadah and asked my father why the Jews were God's chosen people. He said, without missing a beat, "Because they're the ones who made him up."

Okay, I got it. If you make up a god, you make yourselves the chosen ones, not the Moabites next door.

My dad had broken free from ultra-Orthodox parents and felt well rid of much of the craziness. Maybe that's why I understand Frank so well—I've been his daughter. Anyway, my dad didn't become a novelist like Frank; he is a Freudian psychoanalyst. So rather than ideas of God-derived right and wrong, I grew up with therapeutic/scientific ideals of healthy and unhealthy. As I grew up, I thought that right choices, what other people might have called moral choices, probably could be derived more or less scientifically through the science of psychiatry and other disciplines.

Then in the mid-seventies I got caught up in the social tsunami of divorce. My parents were of the first wave, before people learned how to deconstruct their families a bit more gently. My mom curled up helplessly from being left, while my dad stormed and seethed upon finding himself cast as the bad guy. There was little that they agreed upon anymore. And it was hard to believe that either of these two people, who were so miserable, could have the right answers to the questions I had.

So this was the first incarnation of my lifelong struggle with the problem of the source of authority for decision making. Somewhere around thirteen years of age I realized my parents didn't have answers. But they were hardly alone—no one really had answers. In my dawning awareness, this didn't mean there *were* no right answers, only that no one could tell me the right thing to do. I had to try to figure it out the best I could on my own. I'd take advice, by all means, but in the end any decisions I made were mine, and any mistakes I made were mine. There were no "What Would Jesus Do?" bracelets for me.

After my parents split (in more than one sense of the word), I felt to a certain extent that I had to raise myself. My mom had once been so lively that to this day the word *vivacious* conjures up a picture for me of Debbie Roth with her head thrown back, laughing, a scarf knotted on her neck *à la française*, her lips painted a carefree red. After the split she stayed in bed sometimes until 5:00 P.M., while the wallpaper peeled and the carpets showed their threads in a sympathy of neglect. My smart, successful dad was just angry all the time—angry at my mother's helplessness, at how tight money was, at how all of us blamed him for leaving her.

So it was left to me, I felt, to steer myself. It wasn't anything I'd recommend going through, but in the end I learned I could do it. One way or another, I was going to get myself a good life, help my mother get better, not repeat my parents' mistakes. It set me up for activism, this lifestyle, because activism is based on the idea that if something isn't the way you like it, you change it.

This and a whole host of other accidents and reasons eventually took me to politics. But politics is where this neat resolution I had come up with meets its limits. It's all well and good for me to make decisions and take responsibility for myself, but when it comes to other people's lives—and after all, politics is about other people—how much does it matter that I'm convinced I'm right?

For a long time I thought it mattered a lot. In my twenties I helped lead antipoverty and antiapartheid marches to stop social injustice. I worked for Democratic presidential candidates because terrible laws would be passed if a Republican was elected. I cared, and I wanted to make a difference. The humility crept in much more slowly than my convictions had.

I started as a campus activist and traveled with my first presidential campaign in 1984, when I was twenty. In those days I thought campaigning meant you went out and fought the good fight, and when it was over and the Republicans won you took a long vacation, then went on to the next stage of your life. Then, finally and somewhat surprisingly, I worked for a campaign that won.

When Clinton won the White House in 1992, I was twenty-seven years old. I thought, *Finally, all these fantastic programs we have will become law—how bright the future is!* And that wasn't wrong, I'm extremely proud of Bill Clinton's presidency. Frank may think that's BS, and it's a shame he and a bunch of other people are so cynical. There are patriots in the White House just as there are in the military.

But the point is that presidents aren't dictators. Just because we won didn't mean we got to do what we wanted. Besides, I soon figured out that "we" had unity only in defeat. The people blocking most of the Clinton administration's early initiatives were Democratic congressmen and senators. When the gays-in-the-military fumble occurred in the first weeks of the presidency and I found myself having to defend things that I personally wouldn't have chosen, it occurred to me that no one had elected me president. "We" wasn't necessarily "me."

My ideas *weren't* the most important thing, it turned out. And when you sit close to power or read history, you see there are few easy answers and every policy has unintended consequence. If we don't know the "right" answer, then perhaps we have to be content to choose the legitimate answer—the lawful one—as expressed through our constitutional process.

And there's a corollary. If I want people to respect the authority of my guy because he was elected, that respect has to be extended to the other side too if my guy loses. So the irony is that in a lot of ways Frank, once a rabid Republican, was harder on George W. Bush than I was. That's because of my lesson in political process, a dull term for something incredibly profound.

I'm a huge fan of democracy. Not the on-paper, hey-there-was-an-election kind of democracy, but the Abraham Lincoln, "of the people, by the people, for the people" kind of democracy. For me Lincoln's phrase expresses what we should be shooting for. Engagement is the answer to how we live together.

Frank

Kathy told me, "If you believe in God, and if the God you believe in has a code of law, then maybe you have the answers. Democracy becomes moot." But she got it wrong. What Kathy doesn't take into account is that not all religion is the way fundamentalist Islam is.

Those of us who believe that, as finite and sinful human beings, we can't know truth absolutely *do* need Kathy's agora. We also need a separation of church and state.

It is precisely *because* we believe in sin that we believe that we need checks and balances and would not want to live in a caliphate under whatever name (say, in the reformer John Calvin's Geneva) or be politically and legally beholden to a given theology. It is one thing to have a scripture and another to believe that any human or political party, whether judge, preacher, or imam, can interpret it with clarity and rule fairly without checks.

God, Secularism, and a New Agora

Kathy

As reasonable (and secular) as Frank sounds above, sometimes when he talks I hear Rush Limbaugh or Bill O'Reilly or some other angry white Christian man. And I'm sure he hears Hillary Clinton or Jon Stewart coming out of my mouth. But we still listen to each other, we still like each other. If Frank and I can believe in each other, then maybe it's something that can get us beyond our more narrow culture wars.

Frank keeps wanting to talk about God. That can seem odd to me sometimes. It's easy, with a lot of the people I hang out with, to have this discussion about action and legitimacy and "the people" without ever mentioning God. Nevertheless, I think it's good that Frank keeps circling back to religion. After all, religion always has been entwined with the notions of group good that we're talking about. Just because we've taken God out of the public sphere in modern discourse doesn't mean that's the way to go.

5. The Devolution of the American Experience

★

Kathy

We were having breakfast at a hotel restaurant in Manhattan. Frank was talking about the polished folks in business suits gliding in and out of the lobby.

"The most pressing issue on these people's plates is what size bonus they're going to get, and then how they're going to spend it so that everyone knows they've got it. In other words, they're creating nothing, using up resources, and giving nothing back, and we're supposed to admire them? Want our kids to be them? In other words, if this is what we want from our best and our brightest, what kind of future can we expect? These guys are carrying briefcases worth more than my son's salary as a lance corporal! They don't even know what a lance corporal is!"

By this point I'd been on the book tour with Frank for over a week and had come to realize that at times he says pretty much the same thing in a number of different, equally dramatic ways, often separated by the phrase "in other words." Up till now I'd been mostly patient and polite, but before I knew it I was saying, "You know, Frank, you're great at expressing yourself, and I'm smart, so I almost always understand what you're saying the first time, and don't need to hear it the second or fourth go-round."

He considered his muffin, then offered with a smile, "It took me awhile to figure out, after I moved to America and started having Jewish friends, that when they're rude, that's just the way they are—they don't mean it in an unfriendly way."

I couldn't help laughing. We were getting to be friends. From then on both Frank and I pretty much could say whatever we wanted to each other.

"Anyway," Frank said, "all I was trying to say before you attacked me was that there's not much to envy in the lives of the people who have 'made it.' Even for those on top, the ground is unsteady. Will they stay at the top? Will their children make it into the right preschool or be doomed?"

"Have I told you about my cousin Amy?" I ask. "She lives in San Ramon, in the Bay Area. She seems to have it all, from today's perspective. She's got a great house in a development with good schools. They have all kinds of nice modern features like the Jacuzzi in the master suite and the swimming pool in the backyard, and they just redid the kitchen. She's got two little boys, a husband with his own business, a time-share in Lake Tahoe, and an annual vacation to Hawaii. She's a director at Yahoo!—that's a job with good status—and she's been promoted recently. She's living the American dream, right? Or not right?"

We're a society that looks good on paper in a lot of ways, but what's it like to live this dream? To keep this whole show on the road, Amy has to get up before the kids and start the long drive to Yahoo!'s headquarters, in Sunnyvale, which takes about an hour and a half in sludge-like traffic. There's no moving closer—a house would be close to $2 million in Sunnyvale, more than twice what she could get for the one she has in the East Bay. Besides, how stable is that Yahoo! job? Worth uprooting the family for? She was made redundant once at Netscape when they closed her division. Like other modern corporations, Yahoo!'s loyalty is to shareholders, not employees. By the time she gets home most nights, the kids are already sleeping. Anything that goes wrong with the house, the kids, or the car during the day is handled by her husband, who runs his photography business out of the home, and that's a lot for him to juggle.

Neither of them can stop working; they couldn't support themselves if they did. They've got a lot of friends, but when do they really see them? They're all equally busy. This is an exhausting way to live—the perks of holidays and club memberships are pretty much necessities because they are so over-stressed. No tinkering at the edges is going to change any of this.

The American dream? Maybe, but not one that feels great to live in.

People pursue material goals out of anxiety about what bad thing will happen if they don't get to a certain level (or stay there), not because of the anticipated pleasure of getting (or staying) there. And people are increasingly worried about how they are doing. In recent polls, the majority of Americans say security is out of reach.[8]

Frank

The evolution of Disney rides strikes me as a good metaphor for what we've become. Since the early 1960s the designers of the Disney rides have been dealing with an increasingly jaded public. In the early rides people had to do *something* to participate, even if only to glance around. Visitors to the Swiss Family Robinson tree house even *walked* for five minutes or so! On the Jungle Cruise a live guide took you for a boat ride where you sat on a bare bench and sometimes got wet. You had to twist and swivel to see fake animals popping up or in tableaus on the banks of the river, and if you weren't alert you could miss something.

A generation later the Pirates of the Caribbean ride needed no guide, and participation boiled down to turning your head right or left. Next came the Haunted House. By now you rode in a pod, your head more or less held in place while you sat immobilized. The pod itself twisted and turned and pointed you at what you were supposed to see.

The Devolution of the American Experience

In the most recent generation of rides you go nowhere. The "ride" is really a huge room sitting on hydraulic pistons that provides the sensation of movement to people strapped into their seats while the story unfolds on a screen or screens, simulating the sensation of motion—say, flying. This position is familiar to us TV- and computer-screen-addicted Americans, who have turned into a nation of obese couch potatoes. Your job is to sit still as the machine moves you. You don't even have to hold on, and you're in less actual danger than a child on an average swing set, let alone an old-fashioned carousel, where there was some connection to reality, maybe even a skinned knee if you lost concentration.

The book trade too has its rides to nowhere. The best-seller shelves are full of books that lay out the new rules for no-risk winning in the game of life, marriage, and work. The Australian television producer Rhonda Byrne had a best-selling book, *The Secret*, in which she said that if you followed her rules, you could create the life you want—whether that meant getting out of debt, finding a more fulfilling job, or even falling in love.

Byrne's rules are these: decide what you want, then think and feel it, and you will get it. It's the law of attraction, or "like attracts like." The law of attraction means that everything that happens to you—good or bad—you attract to yourself. No one is responsible for anyone else in this world. Whatever bad thing happened, they brought it on themselves.

But there is a problem with this resort to wishful, faith-healer-type thinking. How does it apply to connecting with others? How will it save our planet? How do you deal with evil—say, in one's own mind? If you want something, does that make it good?

Kathy

The faltering of the old American dream, the fact of rising wealth without rising well-being, has been put under the microscope in the last few years by economists, scientists, and social scientists. The modern era was supposed to bring a rational approach to life, to make us all materially better off, to personally empower each of us, and thus to make us happier. But a number of investigators from across the disciplines have pointed out that there is a lot of distress in modern life, or what Yale political scientist Robert Lane called "the loss of happiness in market economies."

Why is it, these researchers ask, that lots of us, more than before, are stressed, lonely, and sad? The good news at the start of the twenty-first century, despite our anxieties, is that Franklin Delano Roosevelt's post–Great Depression consumer economy has succeeded beyond its proponents' wildest imaginings. About half the country was poor in Roosevelt's day, and not just because of the Depression.

Before the modern period, most of the populace of *every* country was poor. We live today in the first civilization in which the majority of people are confident from day to day that their basic needs will be met. We live longer, our diet is better, even the working classes travel for vacations, most people own their homes, and most Americans own cars, TVs, and all the other modern conveniences that their grandparents could hardly have imagined. This is a great success by any standard.

Speaking of Disney, it's as if some exhibition about the future had come true, a sort of never-ending diorama where in each scene the family becomes wealthier: iceboxes giving way to refrigerators, a single phone supplanted by multiple phones, the phonograph superseded by electronic portable entertainment, the typewriter replaced by all-in-one business centers, and so forth. But few people actually *feel* rich. Each luxury in turn becomes a necessity because the whole society moves up en masse.

All the median-income families interviewed in one 2002 study had recently purchased either a new car, a powerboat, a wide-screen TV, a three-bedroom vacation cottage, a swimming pool, or an expensive family vacation.[9] The survivors of the Depression, just glad to hang on to their home and a little simple furniture and a few cans of mediocre food, would think paradise had dawned. And if you sit most people down, they'll usually acknowledge that compared to the rest of the world, compared to our history, we *are* well-off. Between 1946 and 1991, personal income increased 150 percent in real, inflation-adjusted terms.

However, over that same span self-reported happiness *decreased*.[10] Ten times as many people suffer from unipolar depression today as did half a century ago.[11] The inescapable conclusion is that something about our modern lifestyle does not lead to well-being or even to mental health.

Since 1960 the divorce rate has doubled, the teen suicide

rate has tripled, the recorded violent crime rate has quadrupled, and the prison population has quintupled. In that time the percent of babies born to unmarried parents has sextupled.[12] Almost five times as many people describe themselves as lonely today as did in 1957.[13] Moreover, in surveys, people report a general sense of unease.

Most Americans now think that the "lot of the average person is getting worse."[14] Most Americans say the country is divided into haves and have-nots, and identify themselves with the have-nots.[15] According to one study, no matter how much money a person earns, he or she estimated that twice as much is required to live well.[16] One-third of Americans say they always feel rushed, one-third feel their lives are "out of control," and two-thirds want more balance; 60 percent want to simplify their lives.[17] And it's worth stressing that these responses are not simply part of the human condition.

A quarter of American adults say they are extremely lonely right now.[18] And steadily since 1960, according to a periodic Lou Harris poll, people feel increasingly helpless and left out of things going on around them.[19] We've had a threefold increase in GDP in the United States without an increase in happiness.[20]

It's a confusing situation, because people are following rules that used to result in a better life. If this worked at one time, why doesn't it work now?

Moreover, even where people feel good about their personal lives, they've got complaints about larger society. People dislike and distrust the government at unprecedented levels, even compared to the Nixon years. This is true across the developed world. A major complaint people have in most advanced democracies is how alienated they feel. It's a conundrum: how to prevent alienation, anomie, in a society of massive crowds.

There's something out of balance in our society. When a problem is so widespread, it's not a personal problem anymore, it's a political problem—it's a problem of and for society. As Betty Friedan said, the personal is political.

6. The Source of Goodness

⭐ ═══════════════════════

Frank

Kathy says that material possessions don't make people happy, but there is a caveat to that. I think the material world and the spiritual are linked in a way that gives the material world meaning.

When I began to go to a Greek Orthodox church (more than twenty years ago) I discovered the spiritual nature of some physical objects—for instance, our icons, or the elements of the sacraments: bread, wine, oil, and water. One of the pleasures I experienced was the ancient physical side to worship. Even to this convert from bare-bones Protestantism, making the sign of the cross came naturally, as did kissing an icon. It was a relief to be part of a religious ritual that had to do with body and spirit rather than just with an abstract theological idea. Without touch and feel, religion had become as cold to me as it would have been to be asked to be a parent and not be allowed to hug and kiss my children.

Sometimes the material world becomes a liturgical part of one's spiritual world. Ordinary life and non-sacramental objects are sacred—if, that is, you look at the world around you as a gift, not a system.

I happen to love my garden (other than mowing) and my old ramshackle 1835 brick home. Genie and I have been living in it since 1980. And we've fixed it up one room at a time. We plant bulbs most autumns so that in the spring there are now many hundreds of daffodils and narcissus growing in bright naturalized clumps across the lawn. Far from getting tired of my home or wanting a bigger or better one, I become more attached to it. Why?

What Genie and I love about our old pile of bricks, mowed weeds, and gnarled "useless" fruit trees isn't the material value. When neighbors tell us how it's grown in value as our area has "come up," I answer, "That doesn't mean anything to me," or Genie says, "We'll never sell."

What makes a place more than the sum of its parts? It's the continuity and memories. My favorite dog is buried here. Genie forgave me after our worst fight here. I prayed for my son's safe return from war here. If some TV crew arrived to do a home makeover, I'd call the cops for the same reason I'd be tempted to punch a plastic surgeon who offered to "improve" Genie.

The Source of Goodness

When I tell Kathy this, she says that my feelings of loving certain material things (because of their spiritual qualities) aren't all that spiritual. She says they are reflected by the new happiness research. But the research doesn't explain (or at least explain to me) Genie's and my sense of the sacredness found in our home.

When Genie and I visited Mindy Evnin in Burlington, Vermont, she took us to her son Mark's room. Mark was killed in Iraq, a place where our son could have died. Mindy had Mark's uniform laid out on his bed. His books were on the shelves. His clothes were in his cupboard. Mindy hadn't changed a thing. I understood why.

When we visited Mark's grave I noticed people had left Marine pins, flowers, pebbles, physical tokens of love, iconic representations of sorrow and hope. When a National Guardsman Mindy knows jogs past Mark's grave every morning, he salutes. Is that silly? Is it silly for me to make the sign of the cross when I think about those I love? Is it silly for a father to hug his son?

After my son was at war, I understood the icons we kiss when we walk into our Greek Orthodox church better than I had before. I'd find myself in John's room running my hands over his books, touching old toys, looking at the posters of his heroes, even once or twice laying a hand on his pillow as if blessing it, while remembering all those nights I kissed him goodnight.

Kathy

For Frank, and for millions of other Americans, the source of goodness is God. The earth matters because it is God's. To some professed believers, the idea of not believing in God sounds like not having faith in anything, not believing in goodness or in right and wrong. Maybe this is at the heart of our red/blue split, and if it is, we ought to think about it.

In 2007, 60 percent of Americans polled said morality requires a belief in God.[21] But that doesn't mean that the remaining 40 percent *don't* believe in morality. The God/morality conflation is something I see when Frank keeps equating secularism with meaninglessness, in the way a young man I once worked with thought devil worship and atheism were the same. So maybe this is a source of misunderstanding. The truth is that virtually all of us, atheists and agnostics included, are people of faith. It's hard to live a human life without having faith in something.

Many of us just feel uncomfortable aligning with any religion or saying we believe in God, either because we never have or because we associate religion with superstition, an old man in a white beard on a cloud, or a motivation to kill people different from you. On notions of God or transcendent truth, language fails all of us, whether we're religious or secular, and the failure of language leads us to misunderstand and distrust each other. So I'd like to ask the 60 percent of Americans who link God and morality to have the humility and compassion to understand that most of the rest of us are on the same path as them.

The Source of Goodness

Here's a thought experiment I've conducted informally over the past several years on dozens of self-professed materialists, or nonbelievers, to show we're pretty much all on the same path. I ask which of these two situations they would choose. In the first, your child is amoral, and in fact does absolutely wrong things in his or her life, but does them in such a way that it can be guaranteed that no one will ever know about it. Your child becomes rich and has enough money to buy you a luxury lifestyle and set your descendants up for generations of trust funds. In the second scenario, your child is a good person morally and grows up to live a respectable middle-class life as a teacher or other inspiring profession, but is not rich and famous by any means. Which future do you choose for your child?

I've never met anyone who was willing to make the first choice. Even though there is no material harm to your family in the first, no material benefit to choosing the second, the moral middle is the universal choice over immoral success.

Most of us, in other words, believe in transcendent morality, a sense of right and wrong beyond our immediate self. That's what Frank and other people attached to a specific tradition of belief have to understand. We are more alike than different.

Frank asks where this transcendent morality comes from. Absent "thus sayeth the Lord," what's the source? Modern people often fall back on a version of the language used in America's founding. When it comes to moral behavior, right and wrong, we simply hold these truths to be self-evident.

And how is that different from what Frank or anyone else has?

Frank

My mother was born in China to American missionary parents. She lived there until she was almost six. For the rest of her life her stories about China have been a touchstone for her. As Mom has gotten older she can't remember many things. She remembers all her Chinese stories, though, and how she was called Mei Fuh (beautiful happiness).

When she was eighty years old Mom went back to China with Genie for five weeks. They visited Wenchow, on the southern coast, the place my mother was born.

Mom and her family lived in a mission compound surrounded by a high wall. Inside were bamboo trees, flowers, and a swing. There was also a mission boarding school for Chinese girls and one for boys. It was the girls' school that was unusual. In China baby girls were often left to die from exposure, and they were never welcomed as were sons. Mom remembers seeing the pagoda on a hilltop where the baby girls were left to the tender mercies of the elements and wild dogs.

Mom lived in a big house that she can still describe in detail. It had two staircases. One led to Mom's parents' rooms, the other to the women teachers' rooms. There were small houses near the wall for the gatekeeper, the gardener, and Wong, the cook. Sometimes parades with enormous dragons passed the compound. My mother did everything with her amah, or nanny.

Mom's parents believed that they were engaged in very real and direct spiritual warfare over the souls of the Chinese they were trying to convert. Their opponents were the demons and spirits the Chinese worshipped. And in the baby girls left to die my grandparents had a daily reminder that not all ideas are equal, that different ideas about what is important produce different results.

For the rest of her life Mom shuddered when she'd smell incense. It reminded her of glancing through a dark doorway into a room filled with terrifying idols and asking her amah why the passage to the rooms beyond was so crooked. Her amah explained: "People believe that demons try to go in to spoil the idols. But they also believe that demons are stupid and can't turn corners. So they make crooked entrances."

In Mom's mind the idol worship was forever associated with the sound of babies crying, little girls just like her who were abandoned to die and whom my mother's parents tried to save. To Mom Christianity in action was demonstrated by her parents' efforts to get to the baby girls before the packs of feral dogs could.

Today in China they have advanced technology. So today they use ultrasound to find the little girls no one wants and kill them "medically." Abortion does what the wild dogs used to do. Is that progress? Is the problem the form of government or people's ideas about themselves?

The Chinese attitude toward women predates the invention of ultrasound. And if China becomes a democracy, nothing will change for women—unless the Chinese begin to believe that females and males are of equal value.

Maybe Kathy is right and—religious or not—everyone has faith in something. That still begs the question: faith in what? Kathy's benign idea that no matter what we believe or don't believe we're all really the same, that faith in God and faith in faith produce the same results is too narrow. Technology and/or political forms may drive change, and may even have an effect on what we believe to be "right" and "wrong," but our ideas about ourselves drive our choices.

Kathy

I worry that the "shared values" you want, Frank, is just shorthand for "what I want." You can say people don't agree with you on abortion and therefore it's a failure of "shared values" that can be resolved only by getting our values correctly aligned—that is, aligned with what you think or what your religion endorses.

There are some things we should all agree on, and we do—they are the laws we obey. Beyond that, we need what Madison called the marketplace of ideas, and not all disagreements have to be settled in the legislature. In other words, you can work to make abortions virtually nonexistent even if they are legal. The marketplace of ideas is an integral part of the agora, and the agora can't survive without it.

Frank

Note to Kathy: You use the word *should*, as in "There are some things we should all agree on." Where do you get the right to use the word should? Who says what we *should* do? Without some moral imperative, there is no should. You cheat! You borrow moral terminology from systems rooted in religion. Make up your own words!

Kathy

Shared purpose can often connect us, though, where "shared values" don't. That's where *should* comes from. Living in the Bible belt, I've been nonaligned on those "moral and religious" ideas you talk about. Some of my best friends have been evangelicals. They find that I don't believe in Jesus, that I'm not a creationist, that I am, unbelievably, a Democrat. We don't even discuss social policy issues; what's the point? But when it comes down to nuts and bolts, we do stuff together, help each other out, put on a bake sale in front of the convenience store for the family down the road that just lost their dad.

When the question is "What can I do?" rather than "What opinions are dear to me?" there is more that unites us than divides us. And "What can I do?" is a surprisingly gratifying question to ask, it turns out.

Frank

Do I hear violins, another chorus of "We Are the World"?

Kathy

I'll ignore that.

Frank

There are only twenty-five miles of air above us, then nothing else breathable for eternity. Ever look up and wonder, what the hell?

Many of us want to believe that there is some cosmic standard that tells us what is good. It's why young men become Marines—to, as my son explained when he unexpectedly volunteered, "be part of something bigger than myself." It's why the ten thousand years of human civilization are also the ten thousand years of religious and ethical development. Can you have one without the other?

Like Kathy, I also believe we can come together, even though I believe that the human condition is constantly and systematically fucked. The great and the good are on one side, and a pile of ashes and bodies is on the other—Leonardo and Pol Pot, Mozart and Eichmann. I don't think there has been any moral progress. However, I do believe that beauty trumps death. Marc Chagall is not *the* answer to Auschwitz, but his art, infused with love, is a more potent rebuke to evil than one more committee issuing statements about anti-Semitism.

The fight between light and dark just takes new forms. As such, it must come as a shock to those who equate technological, political, and educational progress with moral enlightenment when it turns out that wealthy university-educated men have been among those strapping bombs to themselves, yelling "God is great," and then blowing up children. What's the point of the liberal-humanist *New York Times* editorial page type of dedication to rationality and reasonableness when a first-class education doesn't fix anything?

It's late and Kathy and I are on some dark winding road in the South (somewhere in South Carolina, I think). We're driving in a rainstorm from one local TV station to another. Kathy has an almost-patient expression on her face, as if she's dealing with a kid with a touch of autism who's just trashed his room.

"Now, Frank," she says, "I know what you mean, I think, but people are going to misunderstand you. You really don't mean, of course, that if your neighbors slowly tortured your wife, children, and grandchildren for four or five years, starving them, freezing them, turning them into lampshades, gassing them, and burying them in mass graves, that you'd put that on one side of the scale, Chagall's paintings on the other, and they'd even out."

"No, of course not!" I snap. "And how typical of you Clinton types to parse the legalistic details of something I obviously meant as an illustration."

"What do you really mean?"

"That humans may have made technical progress, but there has been less moral progress. And that I still find hope in beauty, love, and creativity nevertheless."

"Really?"

"Okay," I sigh, "so-called canons of greatness aren't 'in' these days. Some people might scoff at the idea of trying to set and then keep up standards of what is good and lasting. But what else do we have to guide us except the collective aesthetic experience of the human race?"

As we drive on I try to explain my idea that each person attempting to start over and discover everything for themselves is a futile, endless reinvention of the wheel. That is perhaps why the "freedom" of the 1960s led to eventual chaos and was soon abandoned as former hippies turned into grasping yuppies. Life just isn't long enough to keep starting over. And anyway, there are no new ideas. "Free love" turned out to just be another way of saying that professors wanted to have sex with their young students and still feel good about themselves.

"In the end," I say, "even revolutionary societies boil down to the same-old, same-old: individuals who believe in having sex, fear death, make things or don't, just like everyone else, just like the people they revolted against. We're forced to begin where others left off. We're forced to take their word about what works or is good, from trusting heart specialists to going with copper pipe if the plumber recommends it."

In a sleepy voice Kathy asks me to explain myself.

"The Metropolitan Museum of Art is an example of an idea that is no longer fashionable but maybe should be," I say.

"The Met?"

"The Met preserves the collective opinion of humanity about what is good."

Kathy opens her eyes and stares at me, then smiles. "Not

the collective opinion of really rich people who wanted to self-aggrandize while the poor suffered in misery?"

"Is that what they teach you in those liberal colleges? No, because humanity preserved and treasured certain objects and not others. Certainly fluke and fashion and 'history' as told by the winners of conflicts is involved. But there's also a real democracy at work."

"Democracy in palaces, no less?"

"Look, the Byzantines lost their wars first with the Western armies and then with the Islamic armies that overwhelmed them. So the fact that sixth-century Byzantine silver plates can be found in the Byzantine gallery at the Met is amazing. Someone buried those plates on Cyprus rather than allow them to fall into the hands of the marauding armies. Someone else dug them up and didn't melt them down for the value of the silver. Someone else loved them. What gets preserved isn't by chance. It's a vote of confidence in intrinsic value. Humanity therefore 'votes' on what is beautiful. And every time I stand in front of those plates, marveling at the young biblical David's perfect anatomy and the sophistication of the artist, or pay up my Met membership dues, I'm casting yet another 'vote' that will—I hope—help keep those plates around for another thousand years or so."

Kathy stops making smart-ass comments, so either she's fallen asleep or she's gotten the point. I'm never sure if I ever convince her of anything. So I talk on into the night in my favorite manner: the unanswered monologue.

"Civilizations rise and fall. The Met 'tells' us that we should be humble, that someday our time will pass, that we'll be remembered—yes, even America is temporary—only if someone cares enough about the brotherhood of humanity to save a few scraps of evidence that we existed. It also tells us that we'll be forgotten sooner rather than later unless we produce a society that speaks in a universal value-laden language. President Bush proved himself to be a total failure when his 'answer' to 9/11 was to tell America to go shopping. But his lackluster response was in keeping with our new American consumer 'dream,' and it wasn't enough."

"Uh-huh," Kathy murmurs. She rolls her head sideways and falls into a deeper sleep.

7. Beginning to Imagine a New Dream

☆ ≣≣≣≣≣≣≣≣

Frank

What do the ancient philosophers and prophets teach about human happiness? What did Jesus say?

Blessed are *the poor in spirit: for theirs is the kingdom of heaven. Blessed* are *they that mourn: for they shall be comforted. Blessed* are *the meek: for they shall inherit the earth. Blessed* are *they which do hunger and thirst after righteousness: for they shall be filled. Blessed* are *the merciful: for they shall obtain mercy. Blessed* are *the pure in heart: for they shall see God. Blessed* are *the peacemakers: for they shall be called the children of God. Blessed* are *they which are persecuted for righteousness' sake: for theirs is the kingdom of heaven.*

I can't help notice that the Beatitudes have a fair amount in common with the ideas advanced by today's environmental movement. Both advocate a two-step process for change. Both say we need to step out of the way and humble ourselves in the face of a greater good. According to both, we need to identify *ourselves* as the source of our problems, mourn over our mistakes (in other words, repent in order that we may then change what we are doing), and then actually change our behavior.

The idea of consuming as a metaphor for life is certainly the *opposite* of Christ's teaching. Pop ideas about embracing what we want because we want it are also the opposite of almost all the ethical teachings from all religious traditions, including Hinduism.

> *At the core of Jaina faith lies five vows. . . . These five vows, which inspired and influenced Mahatma Gandhi, are non-violence* (ahimsa), *truthfulness* (satya), *not stealing* (asteya), *sexual restraint* (brahmacarya), *and non-possession* (aparigraha). *One adheres to these vows in order to minimize harm to all possible life-forms.*[22]

The Jewish tradition is also clear on the need to act morally, not just grab for what we want. The *Koheleth Rabbah* tells this story:

When the Blessed Holy One created the first human beings, G-d took them and led them around all the trees of the garden of Eden and said to them: "Behold My works! See how lovely and commendable they are! Pay heed that you do not corrupt and destroy My universe, for if you do corrupt it, there will be no one to repair it after you."[23]

If consumer choice is our national purpose, then it's no wonder that people begin to see their lives as rather meaningless and treat everything, including each other, as just another choice. Stay married for the children's sake? Why bother? Maybe there is a better new wife or husband to be had. Another church? Another car? Another planet? That's where the analogy breaks down. There is no other planet.

Kathy

The link Frank makes across religions may be a good place to start when looking for the rock we need to stand on. Going back to the founding of the United States may also be a place to find common principles that can begin to serve as a common bond.

"We hold these truths to be self-evident" may be as close as we get to a national religion—and by "religion" I mean an authority for values that transcends individual opinion— shared by 90 percent of us at least. Why self-evident? Despite neuroscience and evolutionary speculation, in the end these convictions are ultimately as mysterious as religion. And all religions are ultimately as elusive and mysterious as secular faith.

The major religions share the tradition by which God is in a very real sense ineffable, as religion scholar Karen Armstrong and others have traced through the various liturgies.[24] God abides outside the human plane, and all language about him (her, it) is approximate; in the end God is not knowable. In Judaism this is underscored by the precept that you cannot say or know God's name; in Islam there are one hundred names for God, and only ninety-nine are knowable. Taoism describes not a Godhead but rather a path with no end, "the Way."

So there is widespread unity of religion on this point: that God is whole and distinct, yet we can't really know or understand God. The gut-level feeling described by many people who identify themselves as atheist or agnostic or vaguely spiritual but not comfortable with organized religion is not that far off from what's found in religion. Most of us intuit that there is more to the universe than we understand; on that gut level, most of us sense there is goodness and meaning in our lives.

If we can all embrace the acknowledgment of man's limitations as a starting point, this may be a decent basis for forging a common bond. Perhaps we can start with the common denominators between religions and nonreligious traditions and agree on some basic points.

First, there is a limit to human knowledge and understanding about ourselves, the universe, and spiritual truth, and this limit to our senses, intellect, and intuition is an excellent basis for humility. Evangelical Christian, Roman

Catholic, Greek Orthodox, Jew, Muslim, mainline Protestant, Hindu, agnostic, atheist, whatever—all of us can be wrong, even about our most deeply held understandings. That doesn't mean we should give up. We should keep trying but remain humble.

Second, if there is one bit of wisdom that virtually all religious and nonreligious traditions agree upon across cultures and time, it is that compassion matters. What many people call the Golden Rule is constant enough that it seems to speak to human nature, spiritual truth, or both.

Just as the sixth-century B.C.E. Jain sage Mahavira said that a holy life requires one to treat all others as they would wish to be treated themselves, Confucius taught that virtue required that one should never do to others what you would not like them to do to you. Likewise, Rabbi Hillel taught that the whole of the Torah could be summarized thus: do not do to your neighbor that which you would not like done to yourself (the rest, he said, is commentary). And Jesus said to do unto others as you would have them do unto you. Unitarians, utilitarians, humanists, and Zoroastrians all agree (in principle if not always in practice) that other people matter. So this gives us two bases for common truth among all men and women: first, humility should underscore our certainty; second, we ought to have compassion for one another.

Our era requires more of us as individuals than any other period has, because we reject outside authority more than people ever have in history. So to enter the future, we need to be able to tolerate conflicting loyalties. For instance, we can think someone is going to hell because he or she isn't saved, but we must still be willing to care about what that person thinks because he or she is part of "us." Or we can think someone is a fundamentalist rube and still see him or her as a fellow American worth sacrificing for.

Frank

Actually, I love Kathy's vision of how we might achieve harmony. I hope it's true. And if I can come to this understanding, anyone can, because I've done my share of exclusionary proselytizing.

I understand how destructive it is to have a message you just *have* to impose on people even when you know it might ruin friendships, even when it might help rip a country apart. And these days I'd go nuts if my secular friends changed into people like me.

Wanting to convert each other is not the way to build a sense of all being in this together. The best thing we can do is explain ourselves to others, but finish a lot of what we say with the words "But I could be wrong," and mean it.

If half of us are waiting for Jesus to "rapture" all true believers and think that the nonbelievers are second-class citizens, that God is just biding His time to gleefully destroy and torture for eternity because they got their theology wrong, no new American dream will be possible. On the other hand, we'll never get anywhere if secularists either concentrate all their efforts on trying to enlighten believers and strip them of their faith or, worse, settle on just talking to like-minded people. So how do we bridge the gap? To begin with, we all need to take ourselves a bit less seriously.

"You know, you feel free to use terms like 'angry white Christian man' and think nothing of it," I said to Kathy over the phone while discussing this book. "You wouldn't be so happy if I referred to you as a 'hysterical white Jewish woman.'"

"You *did* call me a rude Jew!" she pointed out.

"How about we settle on 'Jane, you ignorant slut'?" I said. We laughed.

Enlightened people always tend to see barbarism in the other but never in their own behavior. Take evangelicals who say that "God is love," then add that He will come back soon and destroy all nonbelievers. Or take so-called progressive feminism and the pop version of it spawned into TV commercials. Do you think it's a coincidence that the stupid fall guy in so many commercials is a guy? He (black or white) can't even buy the right laxative without screwing up. His wife or girlfriend must straighten him out.

We all get used to our knee-jerk prejudices, be they theological Jesus-saves or postfeminist, politically correct men-are-dumb-slobs dogmas. We are so sure of our own civility that we just don't know how rude we really are, even in amusing small ways.

We were talking on a conference call. Kathy was in London, our editor, Elisabeth, was in New York, and I was in Massachusetts. "There are lots of readers who don't believe in God," said Elisabeth. "They'll think you're saying they're bad people because they aren't religious."

"I'm not always sure *I* believe," I answered. "Why would they take offense?"

"It still sounds too judgmental, as if you are saying they can't have values unless they share your beliefs."

To comfortable atheists you are either religious or secular. What happens if those sort of categories are too simplistic? We have gotten used to black and white, faith or not, red state or blue. But some things aren't that easy. Maybe it's time to extend the courtesy of complexity to others.

When I went with Kathy on our *AWOL* book tour, most bookstore managers never associated me with the Frank Schaeffer who also writes novels. In their minds authors who write favorably about military service (as I did in books such as *Keeping Faith*) can't possibly be the sort of person who also writes literary novels.

"Where are my novels?" I'd ask, looking at the book table.

"What novels?"

"*Portofino, Zermatt, Saving Grandma, Baby Jack.* . . ."

"Are you *that* Frank Schaeffer?"

The red-state/blue-state divisions run so deep that you can jump from one stereotype to another and no one makes the connection (even post-Google) because most Americans live in willfully hermetically sealed ideological bubbles where they talk only to their own kind. And people hate being asked even to consider listening to opposing views.

When in late 2007 the *New York Times* announced it had hired William Kristol as a columnist, lefty bloggers went into hysterical paroxysms at the idea that someone from the unwashed neocon mob would be allowed to sully their breakfast tables. No right-wing fundamentalist Christian could have made a better spittle-flecked denunciation of a heretic than some self-styled inclusionary, open-minded lefties when denouncing the *Times'* embattled editors. All that was missing was a stake and a few bundles of wood.

So, Kathy, there's no use calling for a new national purpose and a new understanding of an American identity (of shared ideas) unless we honestly face what divides us. It's about ideas of theological purity (secular and religious), not forms of government, not process, not lack of "connection."

What has divided us is serious. *Roe v. Wade* and the other battles pitting one form of ideological/theological purity against another—from gay rights and sex education to creationism—have given us more than thirty years of culture war. The tragedy of divisiveness cuts right and left. There is plenty of fault to go round.

The Democratic and Republican parties have mostly limited themselves to candidates who are rigidly correct on their social issues. Kathy's friends on the left have made the same mistakes we fundamentalists made on the right. An organization such as MoveOn.org seems just as intent on poisoning the national well of discourse as we nutcase right-wingers-for-Jesus ever were back in the early days of the religious right.

What unites us all is our mutual hatred. For the moment this hatred is still mostly expressed in words. But—and maybe Kathy will say I'm nuts, and I'm sure Elisabeth will—I think that on a long-term trajectory, our war of words could well become our own Shia-versus-Sunni war of bullets. After all, I think some of my father's writings, for instance *A Christian*

Manifesto, inspired a few deranged people to bomb abortion clinics. And we've already had terrorism from the left, from the SDS to the Weathermen. There is no reason to think it couldn't happen again.

But what if slavish intellectual consistency on any issue, from the left or right, religious or secular, is an indication of mediocre intelligence and a lack of honesty? What if what we need to do now is find a way to put the pieces back together for a greater good than our side "winning"? What if our various theologies have blinded us to a far greater and overwhelming set of challenges? What if we need a bigger vision?

My best experience of a bigger vision was my life as a Marine's father. At one time I would have laughed if told I'd be wearing a "My Son Is a Marine" pin or flying a small American flag on my gate, let alone inwardly thanking whoever it was who put up all those flags fluttering on freeway overpasses. I've never been a bumper sticker or flag-waving kind of guy.

John's going to war in two back-to-back deployments was the last step in a series of events that dragged me off my high horse of indifference about who serves and who doesn't, and also about why we *all* need to think of ourselves as Americans rather than members of separate tribes that loathe the "other." Rest assured: whatever my views, I wasn't asking John to check out his fellow Marines' ideology. I was just grateful they were watching his back, whomever they voted for or whatever they believed.

While John was at war I kept a diary. I recorded one incident that seems to sum up my journey into a new understanding of what it means to serve one's country. Put it this way: a greater sense of community was forced on me.

October 22, 2003

5:33 A.M. Angels come to me sometimes. Mr. George Duffy is one. He drove down from Seabrook to get a copy of Keeping Faith *signed yesterday afternoon. As his car pulled into the drive I noticed the front license plate was one of those POW plates New Hampshire issues. I recognized the grandfather of a girl who was in John's eighth-grade class. For a few minutes we talk IC Pelican basketball. Memories flood back. . . .*

Genie, Mr. Duffy, and I stood talking. I asked him about the POW plate. Mr. Duffy was in the merchant marine during WWII. The Germans sank his ship off the coast of South Africa. The surviving crew was picked out of the water. The prisoners cruised around with the Germans for a few weeks until their ship docked in Indonesia. Then the captured Americans were handed over to the Japanese. They were shipped to a hellish POW camp in Japan, where nineteen died.

When Mr. Duffy got home after a year of POW "life"— beatings, torture, malnourishment, and seeing his buddies dying one by one—he found he was "dead and buried," as he put it. Life insurance had been paid out and a memorial service held. Mr. Duffy told Genie and me this story in a matter-of-fact way as we stood around in our kitchen.

I got up this morning casting around for something to

lean on. The war seems to have penetrated my soul. Today I'll hang on to Mr. Duffy and his humor, humility, bravery, and survival. There are Americans who love John and are praying for him even though they never met him. Some of them have faced war too. Other Americans will sleep rough tonight so I can sleep secure in my bed. They are not the people I've spent my life clawing to get next to, "useful contacts" for a writer to know.

My illusion of independence is gone. Being a privileged American living in the twenty-first century has not saved me from a small taste of the emotions that Mr. Duffy's mother felt in 1945 when she thought she'd lost her son. She seems to be whispering, "For better or worse, welcome to the human race."

I also know that the consumer-choice American dream looks like trash when it is touched by life-giving sacrifice, as does ideological warfare between Americans of all persuasions when we look up and realize that we are confronted by serious realities—war, terrorism, educational meltdown, lack of connection to our political system, environmental disaster, cynicism—that demand unity of purpose. The America that worked in Mr. Duffy's day was about building something for others. The question now is what that essential something is for us.

8. History Unfolds and We Respond

Kathy

We may bemoan our consumer-choice America, but we chose it. It was, in fact, a clever response to industrialization and the growing conflict caused by the division of Americans into capital and labor—owner and worker.

A hundred years ago, industrialization grew and spread; it couldn't be rescinded, although there were many people who tried. It was a possibly fatal threat to both America's early Puritan beliefs and rights-of-man ideals as declared by the Enlightenment philosophers. It made the American dream— that is, the first American dream, of self-sufficiency— impossible. Even more, it seemed to threaten our democracy.

The question was this: if the few who own without producing are diametrically opposed to the many who produce without owning, then on what basis can we have enough unity to remain a republic?

America had decades of unrest and real uncertainty about the future of our country during this shift around the turn of the past century. Labor unrest, the rise of radicalism and violence, and communist and authoritarian movements were all in response to the upheaval.

The changes wrought by industrialization affected segments of the population differently. The gap between rich and poor grew precipitously, becoming bigger than it had ever been in any time in our history . . . until today. That gap was growing not because the poor were worse off; they weren't. Rather, much like today, the rich were positioned to take advantage of the changes, which made them richer than ever.

This shift from the old to the new brought so many changes—it shifted the stage from the local to the national; the owner to the worker seemed to bring us to the threshold of losing our democracy. Clearly we no longer regarded ourselves as equals. People were no longer seen as self-possessed on the basis of their economic independence or their moral character but rather as owned and manipulated. How could America remain America? What story could we tell ourselves now?

In 1912, Walter Weyl (economist and cofounder of the *New Republic*) was one of the first to come up with an idea about how we could build a "New Democracy" out of the warring classes. He laid out his argument in a book with that title. Weyl argued that the producer is only the consumer in another role. Where once men were all on common ground as producers (and saw their interests in their productivity), now all men are on common ground as consumers, whether they were called "owners" or "laborers."

This new formulation was an enormous shift from our previous idea of how one best lived. In the Puritan- and Enlightenment-inspired era, freedom meant self-sufficiency. Work bred character, and consumption was to be moderated, disciplined, or restrained. In this new consumerist era, by contrast, consumption was to be celebrated as the basis for a national identity. And if consuming was an identity—in fact, the key American identity—then politics must reflect that, focusing on how best to satisfy people's "preferences," not on how to restrain them or elevate them morally.

Political philosopher Michael Sandel tells this story and calls this the rise of the "voluntarist" concept of freedom. The idea was that choice or self-expression makes us free, as compared with the original American republican concept of freedom, which was that responsible self-sufficiency, based on character, made one free. This distinction above all others is what reshaped our concept of the good life, which went from being seen as a moral life to being seen as a material life.

The economist John Maynard Keynes articulated the new consumerist reality best. Keynes said that if we reshaped our understanding of economic man away from the owner-or-worker model and instead recast him as part of the brotherhood of consumers, then everybody wins. By focusing on consumerism, Keynesianism paved the way for politics to sidestep controversial issues, such as the moral character or religion of our citizens.

Moral character, with its connection to various churches, where this moral character was supposed to be taught, had become thornier as the country grew larger and more diverse religiously and culturally. Instead of unity through shared morality and religion, Keynesianism inspired the idea that essentially government could focus on simply giving shoppers what they want for less.

Beginning in the Depression Roosevelt embraced Keynesianism with a policy of deficit spending designed to boost the purchasing power of consumers. In 1944, a Roosevelt administration official was explaining, "By freedom I mean essentially freedom to choose to the maximum extent possible."[25] It is the modern expression of the idea of freedom that still resonates today.

The American dream of this new era, early modernism, was of a house and a car, a chicken in the pot, a job with a pension—security and comfort in exchange for working hard. And for a while it worked splendidly. Government policies made that possible, from the social safety net to the tax deduction for mortgages. Beyond dreams of consumer goods, our purpose shifted from livelihood independence (which was no longer practical) to self-expression and self-fulfillment. Ideals of self-expression and self-fulfillment led to the championing of individual rights, expanded the new freedoms to more and more people. One lived this American dream by achieving financial security and by expressing oneself.

And it was good for a long time. But eventually and within

our generation, this "individual purpose" came with less and less connection to any national purpose, other than the fact that the U.S. economy is based on consumer spending, so we need to *keep spending* to keep the status quo.

Frank

A radical view of personal choice—the Weyl/Keynes model carried to its most extreme conclusion—makes us unhappy *and* it isn't good for our earth. It's ugly too.

There are lots of examples of this ugliness, both personal and public. Let's start with one example of consumer choice run amok: the plastic and paper packaging that enshrines things such as razor blades, deodorant, and soda. This isn't tolerable anymore. To call earth-destroying packaging a "private choice" made by corporations and to believe that they have a "right" to make this choice and that our right to buy into it is an expression of our freedom to choose is insane.

And what of other so-called personal choices? How is consumer choice as a life ethic working out for us?

When I walk around New York, Boston, LA, and many other of our swankiest cities, I can't help but notice many rigid faces that remind me of the frozen look my grandmother wore in her coffin—made-up, glued, stretched, and plasticized. Why are so many women (and more and more men) having what is obviously terrible plastic surgery, if one's definition of good surgery is a natural look? I think I know. They don't only want to look younger, they also want to be *seen* wearing a look-I've-had-work-done badge.

The reason for these makeovers is the same reason that some people choose to drive giant SUVs or build 15,000-square-foot homes. If meaning and national purpose are sought in individuals' choices, expressed through being a good consumer, then one must advertise one's choices on the most noticeable scale possible.

Kathy

Many of our problems today seem to stem from the fact that we are playing by rules made to fit an old, failing system. But the fundamentals of our society are shifting. Our culture, our lifestyles, and our American dream (based on market forces and consumer lifestyles) are products of the era that has ended, the age of Modernity.[26] Modernity came in the wake of industrialization; it went out in our lifetime, when America moved beyond postindustrialism and postmodernism and into a new era that has yet to be named.

Frank tends to see the drifting in society today in terms of people losing their way—the flock being lost, as it were. Maybe. But I see a system that once made sense and worked, though it's not working now. We follow it and are still attached to it because we had success with it in the past era. But society, once again, has changed. What remains to be seen is what our response to this change will be.

9. Lessons from a Village

Frank

Maybe we need to look back and learn from successful and sustainable cultures before we look forward. When I look back, I see the Swiss village I grew up in. Even in the 1950s, the higher up the mountainside one lived the more old-fashioned; some might say backward, everything was. And our village was fairly high up our Swiss mountain.

Huémoz nestles midway up the steep foothills rising from the Rhône Valley, below dark forests that end abruptly about two thousand vertical feet above the village, under rocky peaks. Little had changed in our village since the 1800s—or, for that matter, since the 1500s. So even though I was born into the mid-twentieth century and lived barely thirty miles from the bustling city of Lausanne, I observed what amounted to medieval peasant life and a literal model of sustainability in balance with the environment.

Everyone in the village knew everything about everyone, from our village whore's latest outrage—she introduced her skimpily clad illegitimate daughter into the business at the village café when her girl was about fourteen—to our village wife-abuser's latest drunken mayhem, from who was born a few months early (if you did the math from the wedding day) to just why the old lady who never spoke had hanged herself when she was eighty-three. (She had once told a neighbor that since no one ever visited her she was afraid of falling and dying in pain and alone.)

Brueghel the Elder's bucolic paintings of peasants working, sleeping, defecating, and/or frantically making merry could have been drawn from the lives I saw as a child: lives lived as they had been in every farming village in Europe since the Middle Ages, a type of life that was, unbeknownst to me, about to disappear.

But when I was a child it seemed that some things just were: the mountains, the cows, my parents' ministry to the "lost" at their mission. And there were people too who seemed to have sprung from the earth fully formed, who just *were*, as constant and immutable as nature herself.

Bratchi the village mason was one of those. Before you built anything you called Monsieur Bratchi, even if it was going to be a carpentry job. Mason or not, he knew everything about building. If you were smart, you took his advice, especially if you were a family of American missionaries living in Switzerland and not much liked by the local villagers because you were foreign and—worse in their view—some sort of religious nutcases.

We were totally dependent on the few villagers who would talk to us in a civil way. Mom would say things like, "Bratchi says we shouldn't put the window there. He says it faces the weather and won't last." "Well, if Bratchi says . . . ," Dad would answer, then instruct Mom or "the girls" (my three big sisters, who spoke French better than my dad) to tell Bratchi that we would do whatever he recommended.

I first met Bratchi when he came to build a new fireplace in our chalet when I was five. He must have been about thirty back then. We lived half a mile up the road from the village center in a big old chalet that my parents had bought in 1954 when I was two, and where they founded their ministry of L'Abri (the Shelter).

Bratchi was small and wiry. He seemed to be made of mostly weather-beaten sinew. He had a somewhat dour face and a workman's thick stubby fingernails. By midafternoon Bratchi's fast-growing whiskers began to give him a Homer Simpson/Nixon five o'clock shadow. Come to think of it, Bratchi actually looked a bit like a nicer Nixon.

I never saw Bratchi laugh. But this wasn't because he was unfriendly. He would sometimes whistle, tunelessly but happily, but only during the cleanup after work. And Bratchi took his trash with him. Even to abandon a candy wrapper in some hidden spot inside a wall that wouldn't be seen again for a hundred or maybe a thousand years would have been unthinkable.

HOW FREE PEOPLE MOVE MOUNTAINS

I grew up watching Bratchi build additions on our chalet and then on the other chalets my parents' ministry acquired as it grew. Because I was home-schooled and allowed to roam free, I could watch Bratchi work from morning until evening whenever I wanted to.

If I broke the silence, I felt as if I were talking in church. We'd spend whole days wherein the only words I heard him speak were "C'est l'heure de mes dix heures" (it's time for my ten o'clock) or "C'est midi" (it's noon) when he went home for lunch.

Bratchi began work at six-thirty, took his bread and cheese break at ten, and walked home at noon accompanied by the sound of the clanging village church bell telling everyone that the sacred time had arrived when schoolchildren went home for lunch with their mothers and fathers.

Bratchi came back to work at one-thirty, worked until five, then carefully packed up his tools after cleaning everything meticulously. Then he'd clean the spot he had used to clean his tools, hosing all traces of cement and sand away. He never left a trace that he'd been there, not a splotch of cement, no empty bags—nothing.

One of the few times I ever saw Bratchi flush in anger was when my mother wanted him to hurry a job. He quietly but firmly said, "Non, il faut faire ça comme il faut." (No, this has to be done the right way.) A better translation might be: It has to be done the way it *has* to be done. There *was* a right way to do things, an I-have-to-do-it-this-way-because-that-is-the-law-of-the-universe way.

The most ignorant or gullible client got the same high

quality of work as the most astute, and at the same fair price. The mortar between bricks was as precise and finished inside the walls as on the visible outside. To Bratchi there wasn't a visible part of a job and an invisible and therefore less finished part. It all was his work.

What Bratchi built stayed built. His buildings were to our village what the Alps are to Switzerland and what Switzerland (before plastic Swatch watches, drugs, and graffiti) once was to Europe: unsentimental and defined by non-negotiable solidity.

Our village was a tight-knit community, with the exception of us Schaeffers of course; I mean the Swiss contingent was tight-knit. Sometimes those bonds were forged from trust. Often they were not. There were many grudges, many cliques.

There were people who never spoke to each other: "She puts her eiderdown and pillows out to air so late, sometimes not until eight o'clock!" "She dirtied the fountain with carrot peelings when she went to rinse out her wash." "He drinks all day and his uncut hayfield is starting to sprout baby pine trees through neglect." Order was maintained not by the police—there weren't any, since our village was too small to rate a police station—but by public opinion and taboo.

Everything had its place and season. If it was spring, the cows were led to the high pastures a full day's walk away, just above the tree line, to graze on the wide flower-strewn meadows below the looming peaks. I always knew when that happened. The dawn's quiet gave way to the sweetly sonorous bells, and I'd leap from my bed and race down to the road to watch the huge brown-and-white cows trudge past and to see which farm boy would now be gone from the village, assigned the job of living with the cows all summer in the farmer's *haut pâturage* (high pasture) barn. If it was winter, pigs were killed and turned into tangy smoked sausages while their blood froze in bright puddles on the narrow dirt roads next to the farms. Things didn't need much explaining. Things were what they were, what they always had been. No one needed the so-called facts of life explained. Work let you live. Sex led to pregnancy for rabbits, pigs, dogs, cats, cows, village girls. If the cows ate the wild onions, which grew on the side of the road near the cemetery, their milk tasted oniony for a few days, and you knew just where their farmer had let them wander. Wine made you drunk. Pine was for building. Beech was for burning. When a family raked hay in the hot summer sun the fact that the mothers of the family worked stripped to their huge lacy white bras was no more provocative than the men working in their undershirts. Farm women were farmers' wives and daughters—in other words, partners—first and females second.

Families were teams. You did whatever it took to cultivate a small plot of vegetables, raise twenty cows or so, milk them, slaughter the pig, and keep chickens, to cut hay, turn it with pitchforks and rakes, load it on the cart, toss it into the hayloft, and then feed it all through the winter to the cows, who patiently chomped on the dried grass and field flowers pitchforked down into their warm, sweet-smelling stalls. The stalls were mucked out once a day and the steaming manure added to the pile that would, in the spring, be spread on the fields whence came the grass that turned into hay that turned into milk, blood, meat, and manure. The cycle always started over, as it had for your father and grandfather and mother and grandmother since time immemorial.

The land around the village was never stripped or clear-cut or used up or degraded. And because for centuries people like Bratchi had built well and to last, "new" was not equated with progress. Quality was what the Swiss villagers wanted, and so much less was consumed than we consume today. Our village was the opposite of a throwaway society.

10. What Makes Us Tick?

Kathy

Bratchi did work that was meaningful to him and made life around him better. He never got the consumerism memo, and so he's a good example of the good that comes from living another way. Frank talks about beliefs molding people's views, and about those views leading to action or inaction. But there are other forces at work that shape us too. It's not only about belief systems. For instance, maybe we're the first masses who have bought and hoarded so much because we are the first who could afford to.

Yes, as Frank says, some things stay the same. But some things change. How people live changes; it gets more complicated. Because one can trace society from less complex to more complex, there is a progression one can describe as movement up the ladder. All human societies eventually come up with language or die. All come up with forms of technology—the wheel, ways to plant, ways to communicate—and governance or die, and in many instances the parallels of development across vast distances are striking. The point is that societies either adopt a model of existence that can be perpetuated and is sustainable or they don't. The question we have to face now is: does the consumer model of American society, and the idea of freedom as self-expression and consumer choice, give us a community that serves us and that we can sustain?

Frank

In my old village the cows are mostly gone now. The peasants are gone. Their chalets are weekend places for their BMW-driving great-grandchildren. Switzerland isn't a European Union member—yet—but the country has adopted the EU's agricultural rules in order to trade. So the old-style farms aren't even legal. (They are judged "inhumane.") In the one remaining farm in my village the cows are housed in a huge new and supremely ugly factory-like building outside the village that meets the new EU standards for bovine legroom.

Bratchi's oldest son took over the family business, then quit. I met him on a trip home, and he said masonry was too hard a way to earn a living. The Bratchi house is empty, though you can still find the remnants of the big sand pile in the backyard.

What Makes Us Tick?

Kathy

Robert Wright in his book *Nonzero* argues optimistically for our society. He argues for complexity, and for the proposition that cooperation is its natural precursor. In other words, humans naturally work together to solve problems. Time and again, cooperation in the face of external competition leads to innovations within civilizations that in turn require a society to become more complex.

And not only society becomes complex, but people do too. We follow complicated plots of TV series, multitask at home and work, learn completely new technologies every year to update our phones, computers, and TVs. And this mental complexity allows the kind of intelligence we need more of today, the kind defined as the ability to hold two conflicting ideas in your mind at the same time. For cultural anthropologists, this increasing complexity is measurable and is a kind of progression.

The story (as they tell it) goes like this. Human societies started a lot like animal societies. But all human societies throughout the globe eventually became more complex. Some aspect of human nature leads us to try to innovate. Some combination of chance, striving, and trial and error leads some person or group to come up with a good idea that ends up making life easier, getting corn to grow better, easing trade, making the roads better.

Each innovation, each change, forces societies to adjust, forces the people in society to find more complex ways to order themselves. If societies don't change to meet the new situation, they die. So they evolve, in ways that make them (and the people in them) more complex.

Particularly great innovations lead to particularly good results. For instance, the ancient Greeks innovated democracy, which seems to have been critical to the Greek's success as an empire. And then in Rome, when governance reverted to hereditary succession after Caesar, things quickly went awry. The Republic of Venice innovated a kind of limited democratic rule that coincided with its remarkable success and influence for eight hundred years, despite its tiny size.

But this story of innovation and change, which sounds smooth and easy on paper—something like the invisible hand moving things along—is anything but. Changing societies is hard, with sometimes violent struggle and with winners and losers. At the same time that there's something in people that pushes for change, there's also something that pushes for things to stay the same. The key is trying to figure out what to change.

Frank

Kathy says: "Particularly great innovations lead to particularly good results." I'd like to rephrase that: "Particularly great ideas lead to particularly good results."

Looking at America (and the world) exclusively through Kathy's technocratic, secularist glasses misses the point. And just as I most certainly have been conditioned by my background, I think Kathy has been conditioned by hers.

What Makes Us Tick?

Kathy

That's a bit cranky and confrontational, no?

Frank

You know I a) like you and b) know I'm full of crap! But to move on. . . .

History didn't begin with the Enlightenment. And the humanity of that movement came from somewhere. The Enlightenment may have taken an anti-clerical turn, but it certainly borrowed the best traditions of Christian compassion (and the language of ethics) based on Jesus' teaching.

Even during the Enlightenment, Christianity had unlikely fans, even among some of the bitterest critics of the organized churches. Voltaire, to whom Christianity was an "infamy," found the influence of faith, Christianity in particular, useful. "I want my attorney, my tailor, my servants, even my wife to believe in God," he wrote, because "then I shall be robbed and cuckolded less often."

For decades history books in American high schools and colleges have essentially omitted a significant acknowledgment of Christianity's vast contributions to Western society. For instance, when today's reporters, journalists, and pundits attended college their history books and professors didn't seem to tell them that it was in countries where Christianity had the greatest presence that slavery was first abolished.

Abolitionist thinking began in the earliest days of Christianity when St. Paul told Philemon to treat his runaway slave Onesimus "no longer as a slave but as a Christian brother." W. E. H. Lecky, a nineteenth-century British historian (and an atheist), showed that early Christians freed thousands of slaves in the Greco-Roman Western world. And centuries later William Wilberforce, motivated by his Christian convictions, persuaded Britain to outlaw slavery in all its colonies in 1833. In America the first abolitionists were predominantly clergymen. (Though, Frederick Douglass said that in his experience of slavery, some of the worst slave owners were the most outwardly religious and "Christian.")

Nevertheless, horrible lapses aside, what about the freedom that women have in the West? Look at where Christianity has had the greatest presence; that's where one finds women having the most dignity. Where Christianity has had little or no presence most women often lack basic rights. One wag noted that if it were not for Christianity, Gloria Steinem would be still wearing a veil.

Who was the first feminist? The Byzantine empress Theodora. She founded the first homes for unwanted children, and also rescued prostitutes and other abused women—

Kathy

Frank—Stop! We get it—Christians, a lot of them—were/are great. But, hey, look, Exodus and Deborah have something to say about women and slavery too. You don't really want to duel over which civilization most saved the world do you? Muslims and Chinese can trot out their firsts too. . . .

Frank

But wait—what of medicine and caring for the weak and defenseless? Gerhard Uhlhorn, a nineteenth-century historian, said, "The idea of humanity was wanting in the old [i.e., pagan, pre-Christian] world."

Kathy

Gerhard Uhlhorn? Where do you get this stuff? You don't want me to pull out Schmuel Lebivowitz do you?

Frank

What did you expect from someone raised by wolves and fundamentalists in a Swiss forest? These rants just break out from time to time! But may I finish?

As big-time American religion has been folded into the consumer society it all too often preaches just more of the same, a vision of success in consumerist terms with Jesus added on as window dressing.

Contrast the prophetic mission of the older churches—

Orthodox, Roman Catholic, and Protestant—with today's personality-cult-driven evangelical churches and their addiction to the consumer "ethic" that's killing our planet. Contrast the Christian day of remembrance and penance—Good Friday—with another kind of Friday. Every year on the day after Thanksgiving, on what we call Black Friday (the day the big retail stores start to "go into the black," that is, turn a profit), millions of Americans line up in the dark, before the stores open, for super savings. Why do we hoard, spend, and gorge? Why is the consumer model of society so alluring, even to people who know deep down that it's destroying our planet, even our happiness?

We're vulnerable because our culture has forgotten an earlier ethic of frugality associated with the Puritans and the faith they tried to live by. We are also vulnerable because of a leftover, and now useless, evolutionary quirk that makes us want more, more, and *more*. It's the same sort of quirk that makes our bodies store fat when we eat too much, so we won't die in the lean months of winter—which of course never arrive in the modern world, so we just get fatter. But it isn't an extra bit of dried deer meat or a few more berries that we hoard, it's globe-destroying stuff that we don't need and that next year, when we replace it all again, will prove that all that stuff we bought last year never made us happy. And this is our "natural" state. We're hoarders by nature.

When we *don't* hoard, it's not by chance. It's because we impose a moral or ethical system of constraints on ourselves. With no moral restraint—say, a belief that gluttony and greed are sins—we're just another pack of feral scavengers.

What Makes Us Tick?

Never before in human history have masses of us been so conditioned into lemming-like behavior when it comes to consumption. Consumerism baptized as freedom. Stuff replacing spiritual experience, love, and community. But the actual state of our planet (and our levels of discomfort) point to the fact that we are waiting in the wrong line outside the wrong places looking for the wrong things—if, that is, we want happiness and a future for our children. And sooner or later one of two things is going to happen: change will be forced on us by scarcity and environmental catastrophe, or we'll choose to change because it's the right (that is, moral) thing to do.

What we are hoarding is not headed for some future museum. What we're buying will survive only because our Everest of trash will take hundreds of thousands of years to degrade in landfills. And we will be hated, not loved, by our great-great-grandchildren because we are becoming the environmental Stalins of the future, something to be ashamed of, to be forgotten, to be lived down.

Moreover, religion has now been harnessed in service of the consumer American dream. I can't help noticing that many people who claim to have a spiritual base are as bad as (or worse than) anyone else when it comes to contributing to the mound of trash burying us. There are notable exceptions that may well point the way for the rest of us—the Christian groups made up of the Mennonite and Amish, for instance. They live an example of a sustainable and benevolent Christian life that is as earth-friendly as it is socially progressive. But, sad to say, many evangelicals believe that there is a conflict between environmentalism and their religious beliefs.

That's because they've long since bought into a right-wing Republican pro-business agenda and blinded themselves to their own religion's most profound teachings on stewardship and moderation. They feel positively threatened even by a discussion of topics like global warming. This wouldn't matter except for the fact that evangelicals are a political force to be reckoned with.

Many evangelicals see any talk about the degradation of our environment as a distraction from evangelism. That's the excuse. But dig deeper and what you find is people grimly demanding the "right" to own and drive their SUV and claiming that giant home as a sign of "God's blessing." In other words, some forms of Christianity in America have bought into the so-called prosperity gospel, which is really just the religious version of the consumer choice model— plus a "Jesus" designed to give you what you want, like some cosmic ATM.

A recent article in the *Wall Street Journal*, "Split over Global Warming Widens Among Evangelicals," summed up this debacle.

> WACO, Texas——*Suzii Paynter, director of the public policy arm of Texas's biggest group of Baptist churches, traveled to central Texas early this year to talk to a local preacher about a pressing "moral, biblical and theological" issue. She wanted to discuss coal.*
>
> *Christians have a biblical mandate to be "good stewards*

of God's creation," Ms. Paynter says she told the Rev. Frank Brown, pastor of the Bellmead First Baptist Church here in the county where President Bush has his ranch. So, Texas Baptists should demand that controversial plans to build a slew of coal-fired power plants be put on hold.

Mr. Brown was not impressed. God, the pastor said, is "sovereign over his creation" and no amount of coal-burning will alter by a "millisecond" his divine plan for the world. Fighting environmental damage is "like chasing rabbits," he recalls telling her. It just distracts from core Christian duties to spread the faith and protect the unborn. . . .

An episode this spring brought national attention to the brewing dispute. [Conservative strategist] Mr. [Paul] Weyrich joined two dozen other conservative Christian leaders in warning that global warming "is dividing and demoralizing" evangelicals. In a letter to the National Association of Evangelicals, they denounced the umbrella group's Washington-based vice president for governmental affairs, Richard Cizik, an outspoken champion of action against global warming. They demanded that he shut up or resign.

The NAE's board backed Mr. Cizik, who has continued to speak out. Combating climate change, says Mr. Cizik, is no longer just for "latte-sipping, endive-eating elitists from Harvard" but a core issue for all Christians. . . .

In speeches at Wheaton College in 1968, Francis Schaeffer, a hugely influential evangelical intellectual who died in 1984, criticized fellow Christians for neglecting "God's creation." Though a conservative, he hailed "hippies" for their attacks on *"the poverty of modern man's concept of nature." His remarks were collected in a 1970 book, "Pollution and the Death of Man."*[27]

There is a horrible irony in a "religious" position that pits God against His creation. What could be more twisted than Jesus' followers turning their backs on the human future? I'm proud of my late father for standing up against the consumerist culture long before any other evangelical leader. I'm also amazed that more than twenty years later, most evangelicals still don't "get it."

11. Countercultures:
From the Met to the Military Base

★

Kathy

America is full of subcultures, little laboratories for how tweaks in social rules tweak peoples' experiences and attitudes. I've seen one of those subcultures up close.

Military base culture is short on monetary rewards compared with some of the high-flying professions, but it's long on different kinds of rewards, which is perhaps why, despite so many disadvantages, starting with the risk of being killed, people stick around. The military culture is a little alternative society that shows some of the potential of community separate from market values.

On the military base there's no shyness about talking about values. Every service member signs on to patriotism; it's part of the job. It's a major reason people stay, because talking about things that matter—out in public, as part of daily life, at work, on the street—feels normal and good.

That base I lived on, in Jacksonville, North Carolina, was hardly peopled by saints. There were always plenty of fires to put out, from credit card debt to deserting wives. But the fact that military families are as flawed as everyone else didn't stop people from thinking and talking about doing better. And here's what I found: when you share space with people and hear reinforcements about ideas of character, virtue, and doing the right thing, it makes life better.

Frank

Like Kathy, I've lived in values-laden subcultures. I attended two private British boarding schools. The people I was at school with told a very different story about themselves to themselves than the meaning-through-consumer-choice-and-rights story we twenty-first-century Americans have embraced.

I was in those schools on the cusp of the sixties, as the Bohemian spirit rose against so-called bourgeois values. There was a convergence of the anti-materialistic ethos of the emerging hippie movement, which rejected the "plastic society," as Jimi Hendrix and many others called it, and the older ethic of the English upper classes, which liked to feign a cold-showers-are-good-for-you no-nonsense asceticism.

Countercultures: From the Met to the Military Base

An icon of consumption and consumerism such as Donald Trump would have been literally laughed at by the people I was at school with, both the hippies and the traditional gentry. And our publications devoted to the lifestyles of the rich and famous would have horrified both groups too, as would TV tours of the garish and overdecorated homes of movie stars.

In those days it was all about going back to nature, not raping nature in the name of self-expression, let alone accumulating tons of stuff in the name of choice. Back then it was the old gentleman in the shabby tweed jacket, the one driving the old, broken-down car or taking public transportation, who often had the "real money." As for the hip crowd, it was the backpacking hippie, with no more than enough money for a little pot and maybe a plate of rice while he hitched through India to "find himself," who was believed to be cool. Groups such as Monty Python mocked the consumption machine with their portrayal of Mr. Big, people who ate up the wealth of the world until they vomited . . . or exploded. Hip or square, one simply didn't boast or flaunt.

"You'll offend some rich readers," my editor says. So let me add this: I'm not saying that there was no hypocrisy involved in such Victorian-inspired and/or counterculture asceticism. And of course the estates of the British aristocracy are what today's crass billionaires are trying to imitate with quantity if not quality. But at least the old British attitudes about modesty (even when hypocritically expressed from the comfort of some grand manor) projected an ideal of life that was about more than accumulation. It also happened that both the hippies and the old-school gentry lived by a code that was more planet-friendly.

Kathy

My kids and I filed into the movie theater just as it was getting dark. The old-style giant screen lit up, and the film rolled on jets screaming off into the clouds. We stopped where we stood and placed our hands over our hearts, and a fulsome instrumental of "The Star-Spangled Banner" played while images of tanks, homecomings, helicopter lifts into the sunset, and camouflage-streaked faces flashed and faded. When it ended, my daughter, eight-year-old Sophie, leaned over and whispered, "That's my favorite part."

I felt a bit goofy the first few times I stood up for this routine. It seemed vaguely coercive and pretty square, not up to modern sensibilities. It's the kind of thing that might have played on Main Street in the 1950s or early 1960s. If it played in the civilian world now, at least in most of the places I've lived, it probably wouldn't last long. Someone would complain about the message as "glorification of the military." But as Frank said to a critic, if we're not willing to hail the military for the work they do, then on what basis should they do it?

Anyway, in the outside world there'd be friction between people who stood and people who refused to stand. Whoever owned the theater wouldn't find it worthwhile to put off some of his customers. So things like the national anthem at the beginning of a movie, a little gesture that can give an emotional ping of togetherness, have gone away.

But we were on a Marine Corps air station. The short film seemed to be celebrating us. You could call it corny, sentimental, propaganda. But it's also inspiring; it buoys you up a bit, makes you feel like you're doing something worthwhile. There's no law that says you have to stand, but it would seem churlish and actually unkind to exercise one's right not to. And, anyway, as my daughter says, the anthem at the beginning is her favorite part.

Frank

Boarding school aside, I've experienced another alternative to consumerism in another community: the community that makes and sustains art. Art provides a bond between people and affirms a meaning to life that isn't always about money. It may be about things—art objects—but they are important to most artists because they are evidence of human expression, not "useful," just as patriotism, love, and friendship aren't useful by bare-knuckle consumerist standards.

Read Vincent van Gogh's letters to his brother Theo or those he wrote to Gauguin. Van Gogh is wrestling with what to paint, where to live, how to work. He's arguing passionately for working from nature, rather than (as Gauguin did) from imagination or mere memory. Issues of color and composition, and of faithfulness to reality while building on that reality stylistically, preoccupy van Gogh.

Certainly some artworks take on exorbitant monetary value—van Gogh's, for instance. And some artists are actually "evangelists" in the sick "church" of consumerism-trumps-all-values we now worship in, as is illustrated by a certain diamond-studded platinum human skull sculpture that sold for about $100 million to a consortium of investors. (The crassness of the work aside, it's been alleged that these were blood diamonds, the kind that leave a trail of exploitation and death across Africa.)

But, a few terminally greedy artists exploiting a few terminally greedy investors aside, most painters, writers, poets, and composers don't do what they do for the money. Most artists—like most of the military people Kathy describes—have been failures when judged from the point of view of what makes a good consumer. Art, like patriotism, like meaning found in community, like family and love, has been about something else besides stuff.

Genie and I stay in a cave on Manhattan's Upper West Side. We think of it as "our bedroom at the Met." It's also my writing room. The cave is a studio apartment just big enough to accommodate a fold-out bed, desk, chair, small round table, and medium-sized carpet. It's on the fifth floor at the back of a chunky old pre-war sixteen-story building on Broadway. The light is used up long before it filters down to the grimy window facing the narrow, tunnel-like inner courtyard. Perpetual twilight suits me. I don't want distractions when I write.

When I'm at the stage of writing a book where I need more than my early morning routine to get the job done, I disappear into the cave for several weeks at a time. I send out for food. Genie stays home in Massachusetts. She visits on weekends.

There is no lawn to cut or snow to shovel or plumbing to repair in the cave. The outer world is the building manager's problem. The walls are bare, so there is nothing to look at. There is no TV, and the laptop I take there is old and slow and does nothing unexpected or entertaining. And Larry next door is kind. He's hard of hearing and so he plays his TV loud sometimes, but he gave me his number so that when I'm writing I can call him and he turns it down.

By midafternoon, when I can't write anymore, when another cup of coffee will only make me feel paranoid—or "even more paranoid," as Genie says—I walk to the Metropolitan Museum of Art. It's the real reason I find so many excuses to be in New York.

By the time I'm in Central Park and strolling around the reservoir on the jogging path, I'm feeling the way I used to when I was a child and our family traveled by train from Switzerland to Italy on our annual summer vacations. Almost nothing grown-up is as satisfying as the memory of those sublime childhood vacations in Portofino. But the Metropolitan Museum of Art is.

What I find there blessedly contradicts both the secularism that is typical of so much thought today *and* the exclusionary fundamentalist religiosity I escaped from. What I see tells me that there is a common thread linking all of humanity.

Brain science and genetics, Calvinist theology, and/or Darwinian psychology say that I don't have free will, that I'm a mere slave to my genes and/or God's will, that even altruism can be explained away, and that maybe there really isn't a "me" at all, no one home observing anything, just a brain fooling itself into thinking it's thinking. The Met holds out hope of something else: that I can look out via my brain, past the science and theology, and touch a spirit that gives me joy. The Met also tells me that being a writer is worthwhile.

The evangelical slant on art and writing is that in itself writing and art isn't worthwhile. It must serve some ulterior purpose. In the evangelical's case this purpose is "bringing people to Christ." Of course, this utilitarian view of art isn't unique to evangelicals. The socialist realism favored by Joseph Stalin or the feminist art of the 1970s was based on the same idea: art is for proselytizing, politics by other means. The Met tells another story: art doesn't need to be justified or make a point. It isn't *about* being human—it *is* being human.

Sometimes religion is the excuse for art, but even religious art isn't about the religious patron or the theology. We forget the bishop who commissioned this or that Madonna and Child. We identify with the artist's emotions expressed through the work, whether we think the virgin birth did or didn't happen. The art transcends ideas about the subject. It just *is*. It exists outside of the artist's intentions. He or she loses control of the work. It belongs to the person looking as much as to the artist. In that way, like reality itself, art is bigger than the artist's ideas about it.

In the Met I can just be one of many: we who look for support from art, from the objects that have interested (and been loved by) humans for millennia. These objects urge, "Keep writing! Keep looking! Keep painting! Keep mothering! Keep fathering! Keep loving! Keep grieving! Keep doubting! Keep questioning! Keep lusting! Keep believing!"

Countercultures: From the Met to the Military Base

Art "says" that human beings are important and that therefore the choices we make are important too. Art says that a good life requires character.

Roman, Chinese, Greek, Japanese, Islamic, Byzantine, American, French, modern, and medieval art all record the fact that character exists—that morality and character have an identifiable meaning for humans across cultures, mythologies, and time. The struggle to become the right kind of person is as real and constant as math or physics. Almost all myths in all cultures are about choosing what is right over what is easy. And abstract art or postmodern non-art art is no different.

Even if the intended message is that absurdity rules the universe, the fact that someone felt it worthwhile to communicate that idea trumps the intended message. In that sense an "empty" Rothko canvas—a "mere block of color"—is as figurative and descriptive as any Rembrandt self-portrait. The mere existence of a Rothko is a self-portrait of the artist too, a reaffirmation of the essential belief in the worth of communication.

And the lasting point of surrealism (whatever the artists intended) isn't that life is absurd but that the human condition is rooted in values so firmly understood by so many people that altering our perceptions has shock value. Nothing affirms the status quo more than irony at its expense.

It turns out that the values that unite humanity make the word *diversity* just plain silly. We are the same. Art is a message in a bottle from the past to the present, and from the present to the future. The message: we matter and we are one.

Kathy

Friends were visiting us once on that base in Jacksonville. They came from the "People's Republic" of Tacoma Park, an ultra-liberal enclave above Washington, D.C. The teenage daughter took in the flag-lined main drag with elementary school, day care center (sliding scale beginning at $35 a week), bowling alley, first-run movie theater charging $1, the hospital (free and open to all), the after-school play and homework center (cost: $5 a year). She looked at the relatively similar houses for staff sergeants and sergeant majors, for captains and colonels; at the kids riding their bikes in groups around the quiet side streets, speed limit 15 mph. "It's like a little utopian community," she said.

Yes, ironically, it's on U.S. military bases that some of the most idealistic tenants of socialism have come to flower. Money is not a big motivator on a military base, since everyone of the same rank makes the same amount of money, and there's a pretty level playing field for advancement. The highest-paid person—say, a fifty-eight-year-old general—makes about twelve times more than the lowest-paid nineteen-year-old private. And there is a bit of "from each according to his ability, to each according to his need." Your house size has something to do with how many kids you have. How much you pay at the day care center depends on how much money you have.

My husband and I are in our forties, pretty old in Marine Corps terms. That makes us among the highest earners, but the social ethic of the military would make it seem terribly gauche to flaunt it. It suits our personalities to drive old cars, but here it also seems more socially acceptable—even though that twenty-four-year-old orange diesel Mercedes my husband rumbles along in is pretty distinctive.

Values rooted in more than material striving may have departed the town square in much of America, but not on a military base. So in the workplace, there are signs to remind people of the virtues. In my husband's old squadron, stenciled on the concrete steps leading from the hangars to the admin space were the words *courage, determination, loyalty, honesty,* and *respect,* a different word for each step. And when there's a medal ceremony or a promotion ceremony, a lot of people come. They listen to words about the meaning of the award, the trust the recipient seeks to live up to, the fineness of his or her accomplishment. There's a lot of emotion there.

The base has a culture of volunteering. When a squadron deploys, it's not a paid admin person or a social worker who plans activities for the families, keeps families informed of the latest doings, or steps in to help out the folks who are struggling, but a group of wives from the unit that does the work. There may be some grumbling about this, but there isn't any money to pay for a hired person, and it's work that has to get done.

In the outside world, there's no way you could expect someone's spouse to do unpaid work to assist her husband's workplace—that would be a bit outrageous. But our world is different. And, it turns out, as a general rule people do better when they are doing for themselves, not passively receiving services. Moreover, the habit of volunteering leads to more volunteering and engagement. It changes you.

People are more likely to volunteer on a base because they get asked a lot; socially, it's not considered an imposition on anyone's privacy to ask. The idea is that we're all in this together. Action begets action, and the first level of taking part usually occurs because someone's asked you. Career military wives, the ones who roll up their sleeves like Rosie the Riveter, are often among the most capable, versatile, and independent people you'll ever meet. The question is, are there ways to export some of these ways of living to the larger culture?

12. The Good of Good

Kathy

"Look, people are rational actors," the guy calling in to the radio station said. Frank and I were on a show in San Francisco. "It's natural to seek pleasure and avoid pain, so it doesn't make any sense to expect self-sacrifice."

The next person on the line was a much older man. "We all wanted a better life too back when I was young; of course that's natural. But we understood that we had to go through something tough to get it. For us it was World War II. No one asked us if we wanted to do it; any decent person wanted to, had to. The good life came later, and we had earned it. It was all the sweeter. You wouldn't take a million dollars to go through what we went through, but having been through it we wouldn't give it up for a million bucks either. That's something people miss today."

After the taping ended we took a break before our next gig. We sat in a sliver of sun on the patio of a narrow walkway off Nob Hill, me drinking a latte, Frank with black coffee, and Frank said, "We should be speaking in nursing homes, because the people who get this issue, who really get it, are the Greatest Generation. Those people lived through pulling together."

"It reminds me," I told Frank, "of my father-in-law."

Clive is eighty-five years old. When he was nineteen he enlisted in the Navy and served two years before the war ended. He's lived a long time: marriage, three kids, divorce, six grandkids, a few careers.

"He told me when he was visiting recently, and thinking back over things, that that time in the Navy was the best time of his life."

My daughter likes to say that her grandpa fought in World War II. But he didn't fight. The war never came to his patch of the Pacific. It makes one think of John Kenneth Galbraith's line, "Never in the history of human conflict has there been so much talk of sacrifice and so little sacrifice." But that's unfair. Nothing bad happened to Clive, but purpose doesn't have to involve pain. The willingness to risk hardship, perhaps, but not always the infliction of pain.

What Clive *did* have was purpose, a sense that he was part of a group engaged in something that mattered for everyone. So here he is now, sixty-five years later, and it shines for him, the sense that he was part of something worthwhile and that he could make a difference. And the friends he made then stuck with him for life too. It's a cliché, maybe, but that doesn't stop it from being true.

The argument isn't that war is good. It's that group purpose has tremendous rewards. A materialist might ask, "Conserving the planet, helping near or distant poor, building structures that might help prevent war—what's in it for me?" And the answer is: do it for the pleasure, for the anticipation of future glory, for your grandchildren.

Frank

In my Swiss village, people lived as they thought right. It just so happened it helped everyone too. And they helped our earth because their life cycle was a sustainable one. It also provided a feeling of solid ground under your feet.

However, the village could not have functioned if people had let their differences, even their hatreds, keep them from cooperating. They might not have been on speaking terms, but when, for instance, it was someone's turn to use the tractor to power the band saw and cut firewood, one "enemy" would hand off the saw to his neighbor, even if they exchanged no greeting.

Kathy

If we're looking for examples of how free people work together, Switzerland isn't a bad place to look. The Swiss may not rock the world there, but they are as engaged as any modern people are with the running of their society.

As it happens, the innovations the Swiss found, hundreds of years ago, to forge harmony and stability out of a country of cantankerous multilingual, religiously divided cantons may offer us something. The Swiss, more than any other country, run their own show, steer their own ship. They have a more direct democracy than any other modern nation (our democracy is mostly practiced through representatives). The Swiss have referendums on certain local and national issues and essentially can recall legislation if they get enough signatures on a subject.

The upshot is that the Swiss coincidentally show the greatest satisfaction with their system, and one of the highest overall levels of individual well-being of any country in the world.[28] And this isn't a small point. Researchers who study well-being see that being part of a society that makes participation possible, and then participating, is part of the recipe for a good life. Maybe we can learn something.

One of the reasons people in America are alienated is that it's very hard to affect our system. There's too much big money and too many people trying to manipulate things. But maybe it's time to reform that. Maybe it's time to note that more participation is better and restructure things accordingly. And perhaps we can one-up the Swiss: use new technology to bring us into even more direct participation in a sort of ongoing referendum on policy.

In the example of Monsieur Bratchi, Frank saw that people who are good for society develop their character, skills, and outlook not in a vacuum but in community with others. And what we call character is not something we are born with but something that is cultivated by what we do. Individuals and society are in an enormous feedback loop. It's not possible to live the best life you can in a broken society, nor is it possible for the best society to be made up of half-people. It's all about how we relate to and treat people. So good feeling is not a cause but a by-product of other factors.

What does modern research tell us about the conditions of human society (as opposed to internal personal characteristics) that improve human well-being? Money matters—or rather, what matters is having enough wealth to be above the poverty level. Then what seems to matter is engaging beyond oneself. Researchers find specifically that the greatest markers of well-being are marriage and organized religion, with close friends and larger social ties not far behind. Living in a participatory society, a democracy, matters, such that the more participatory the democracy, the greater the well-being. Moreover, researchers find that when people have positive purposes, they thrive.[29]

As we seek to change ourselves, change the way we connect on a large scale, we can be reassured by these findings: if we can find our way to engagement, to large-scale connection, then not only may we create the means to meet our era's greatest challenges, but we may find our greatest personal satisfaction too. The old pop songs are right—love is the answer.

These conditions don't happen *to* someone. They are things that require participation and good choices, and a certain amount of character and energy.

I'm a big fan of the Jewish concept of mitzvah. A mitzvah

is a duty, a good deed you do, a commandment (Frank—you'll like that word!). But it is also the blessing you receive. Doing the good deed doesn't bring a blessing—it's the good deed itself that *is* the blessing. And that's not all: the word mitzvah also means "connection." The act is a connection to God, and if the deed involves another person, it is a connection to that person.

Duty, good acts, blessing, connection: all facets of the same stone. In many ways this one word sums up much of Frank's and my thesis. And indeed, this insight proves true in studies of altruism.

Doing good is its own reward, in both body and spirit. Mitzvahs not only help the people directly involved, they create widening circles of good; they strengthen society. People who are engaged have demonstrably more social skills, which make it possible for them to build and sustain communities and hence the larger society.[30] In this sense, the good feeling that comes from purpose and connection can be said to have evolved as a positive attribute in our ancestral home: happiness and cooperation reinforce each other, and cooperation leads to group survival.

Doing regular volunteer work, especially while interacting with others in a warm and compassionate way, dramatically increased people's life expectancy and vitality.[31] Elderly patients who volunteer have improved health and longer life one study found.[32] Harvard graduates who have an altruistic lifestyle are more likely to have good mental health than their less-giving fellow alums (as tracked by a study over thirty years).[33] And scientists conducting a study sent out college students in two groups, one to indulge in a pleasurable activity and one to do good deeds. The study found that the "Samaritans" experienced a greater and longer-lasting mood lift than those who were tasked to get immediate gratification.[34]

If you serve your family, your friends, your *métier*, and your country and they serve you, that's a good start. "All for one and one for all"—Switzerland's motto, in fact—is a recipe for well-being. It's been shown that people thrive when they feel both that they can direct their own life and that they can contribute to something bigger, in particular to their society.

13. Making a Great Generation

Frank

My father-in-law Stan is a good example of someone who affirmed his life by being part of something bigger. The word *mitzvah* was not one I ever heard him speak, but Stanley Walsh lived mitzvah. He was a member of what Robert Putnam called "the long civic generation." Stan was a big man, tall, well built, and strong, with a big, fleshy, friendly face. Stan looked *out* at the world through clear eyes, not inward.

Stan served during World War II. He belonged to clubs. He voted. He worked for candidates. He volunteered. He worked through various groups to spread general knowledge, for instance, being a driving force in the California Map Society as well as in the California Bar Association. And Stan was also incredibly kind to a certain terrified teenager who got his daughter Genie pregnant. For Stan that kindness, as well as social and political involvement, was all just normal life. But what made these things possible was character, better understood in the context of a private life well lived.

When Stan decided the time had come for his evening cocktail, a trip to a particularly beloved supermarket, lunch, dinner, or any other appointment, he didn't like to be late. And once Stan decided that his time to die had come, he refused further treatment for his cancer, called his priest, said his goodbyes to his family, and asked that he not be fussed over. He refused medication that would have clouded his mind, preferring to face his passing unflinchingly.

In his final illness, Stan did not want to be pitied. He would not have known what to do with anyone's maudlin sympathy. As he told his granddaughter (my daughter, Jessica) when she called him just before he died, "I don't want you to be sad. I've had a good full life." As he put it to his daughter, my wife, Genie, "I'm good with God." That was about the most any of us ever heard him say about himself.

Stan was a man of great achievement. But during the thirty-four years I knew him he made it very clear that the achievement about which he was most proud was the fact that Betty Jane King married him. All of Stan's friends, career, and many associations can be understood in a single phrase: what made Stan tick was his love for his family. This extended to a sense of duty to his community and his country as the place his family lived, and therefore something to be nurtured and, where possible, improved. In a way, that is all one needs to know about Stan and the generation that made America a great world power: love and commitment were the bedrock upon which their lives were built. Another shorthand version of Stan's life is this: he lived the American story.

Stan's mother, Margaret McShane, came to Kensal, North Dakota, as a homesteader and built a sod house on the open plains along with several of her siblings. Stan's father, Tom Walsh, was the town's blacksmith and first baseman on the semi-pro town baseball team. At the age of seven Stan lost his mother to a childbirth gone wrong in which baby and mother died.

Stan attended the University of North Dakota, arriving in September 1935, at the height of the Great Depression. He had one pair of boots and $15 and went to school without any means to pay the tuition. Stan earned his keep managing university functions while also becoming president of his fraternity. He couldn't afford to live in the dorm and slept in an abandoned railroad caboose along with five other impoverished students. They referred to their so-called dorm as "Camp Depression."

Later at Georgetown Law, Stan was still too poor to buy books. So he completed his law studies using Library of Congress books, which he was able to borrow because of the kindness of one of his state's senators. Stan graduated at the top of his class in 1946. Then he was a professor of law at the University of San Francisco from 1946 to 1951. After that he practiced law until his retirement in 1990.

Stan's listing of "significant college activities" (something his family discovered in some old papers after he died) shows that even as a student he was already a gregarious man who had wide interests and enjoyed socializing. He was a joiner and participator. There is a long list of social, scholarly, and benevolent organizations to which Stan belonged: a fraternity, several charitable societies, and two debating societies.

Stan's ability to join groups was the opposite of excluding the "other." Stan was especially proud of his 100 percent Irish Roman Catholic ancestry, but that didn't stop Betty, a Protestant American blueblood whose ancestor Rufus King signed the Declaration of Independence, from marrying into the recently arrived Irish Walsh family.

Kathy

In his well-known study sociologist Robert Putnam finds that we've lost "social capital," as he calls it. He cites four reasons for this loss and assigns percentages to each based on their importance: 10 percent due to the pressures of time and money on two-career families; 10 percent due to suburbanization, commuting, and sprawl; 25 percent due to TV and other electronic entertainment that provides an easy alternative to socializing; and a whopping 50 percent due to what he calls "generational change," or the aging of the Greatest Generation.

Generational change is another way of saying that as the generation born between 1910 and 1940 retires and dies, no one is replacing them in doing the work of holding our country together. This "long civic generation" is responsible for most of the social capital in the country, most of the joining, volunteering, serving, stepping up. Why did this group do more at every stage of their lives? Did they have more time? No, they were as busy as today's thirty-year-olds. So why did they step up? Well, they had more training.

Most of this group had military service, which was valued by their society as a gift to the country. Those who served during Vietnam didn't come out having learned the same lessons of engagement or having experienced gratitude from others. The legacy of that era was alienation and division, the start of the culture wars from which we have yet to recover— wars Frank and I are asking our readers to set aside.

Frank

The idea of a culture war was utterly foreign to Stan. You just didn't hate people or divide yourself from them because of contrary ways of seeing things. As for the self-reinforcing habits of today, of reading only blogs by people who already agree with you, Stan would have been bewildered. He *liked* to be challenged. He *liked* to meet, talk with, or read books and articles by people he didn't agree with. He knew what he thought. He was secure. What was the point of living in an ever-narrowing echo chamber?

As part of his Irish heritage, Stan held his Roman Catholic faith close. But Stan was not one to proselytize even though he made it clear that when he talked about church he meant the Roman Catholic Church. He was devout, but somehow that didn't mean that Stan thought less of people who were not.

When Genie married me, Stan knew that I wasn't just any old Protestant but (back then) one of that fearsome sort of evangelicals who regard themselves—and only themselves— as the "elect." And I was from a missionary family that had first gone to Europe to convert Roman Catholics (among others) to our kind of "real Christianity." We were the sort of believers who, in my parents' early unreconstructed fundamentalist days, declared people like Stan to be in need of salvation and labeled his church the "whore of Babylon." Moreover, I was involved in the emerging religious right, and Stan was a life-long Democrat. But Stan was a live-and-let-live sort of guy. He knew who he was. He wasn't threatened by welcoming a very different sort of son-in-law into his family from the one he had no doubt hoped his daughter would marry.

Just after my son John joined the Marines in 1999, he got a call from Stan, who gave him a heartfelt "We're all so goddamned proud of you!" Coming from his admired grandfather, those words meant a great deal. John's eyes lit up when he reported what Grandpa Walsh had just said. It was as if God had pronounced John's choice to serve his country good and right.

This was in stark contrast to many of John's friends on the North Shore of Boston—and especially their parents—who regarded military service as some sort of second-best choice, something reserved for those with "no other options," something their kind no longer even considered. But Stan was of the generation of Americans that—Democrat or Republican, religious or secular, left or right—*expected* people to serve their country without a second thought.

Making a Great Generation

Kathy

Frank is describing a model of what America must be, a place where red and blue can disagree, a place where religion can really matter, but not more than other people. If we're trying to find our way to the promised land, an era where we can build a new agora, where we can match our personal purpose to the purpose of the day, where we get another shot at Eden, then we need to find models to emulate.

People like Stan Walsh are one kind of model. And there are others. Because all around us is a new potential Greatest Generation, or at least one working at making things better. The motto of this new group of people may well be the motto of a group of young engineers at MIT and elsewhere who've given themselves the challenge of building the first super-efficient vehicles: "We are the people we have been waiting for."

Our country breeds hardy perennials, and everywhere you look there are people moving past the old model of consumerism and individual rights and toward a truly creative engagement. In many ways these are our new pioneers, building their own versions of that sod house Stan Walsh's mother built, doing good not only for others but because it makes their own lives better.

I met Greg Mauro back in 2000, when I was doing a bit of work for the Gore/Lieberman campaign. He was a thirty-year-old private-equity guy, a former Silicon Valley roommate of some of the founders of Netflix and eBay. When he wasn't making deals to form new tech companies, he was out off-shore surfing in international waters near Indonesia or helicopter skiing in Canada.

Once or twice he invited me to parties at his place in La Jolla, where you could go up to the roof deck on the Fourth of July and watch three different sets of fireworks explode off three different beach views—that is, if you could see around the Russian models leaning on the balcony. He sounds like one of these guys Frank rails against, doesn't he?

But he isn't. We stayed in touch because even though politics ultimately turned him off, he kept calling me about ideas he had. He cared a lot about the school system being screwed up, and eventually got involved in charter schools, joining the board of an organization I'm a big fan of, High Tech High. He's raised over $35 million to help build a number of additional schools.

Greg's in his thirties. He has no kids; he's not married yet. He's not running for office, and he doesn't have a PR person (other than me, apparently). He's not mega-rich. Not hurting, for sure, but he puts a lot of his money into creative good works. He's got other ideas too—about prisoner rehabilitation, for instance, and providing mobile phone access in the third world. He likes to bounce these ideas off me, and I like talking about them.

Greg was in London to pitch some business in the City and we met up at a pizza place across from Hyde Park. "So why do you do these things?" I asked him. "Plenty of other people in your position don't. Where does it come from?"

And what he answered boils down to the idea that he'd basically be ashamed of himself if he didn't. His actual words were that he'd feel like a parasite. Why does he feel this way when others don't?

Frank will love some of Greg's reasons. For one, he's Roman Catholic. I've known Greg several years, and I didn't know that about him until we talked about why he does what he does for other people. I think that probably most of his friends don't know. Greg doesn't go to church that I know of, but it's how he was raised: his mom was involved in the church, and she taught the kids to give back.

Greg admires his mom, and so that's a factor. Frank will love this too: before college Greg spent a year in Europe at a Swiss school studying art history. Art history was eye-opening, a link to the human side of history.

So Greg knows he's got some talent, certainly a talent for putting together people and ideas to make companies. Because of the way he was raised, he understands that talent not to be his personal property, a thing he "owns" and can dispose of how he wishes, but to be a gift, something to be grateful for. And therefore this is his reason: he owes something back. Plus giving something back is gratifying. It makes his life better. He's a happy guy. He's a good example of how obligations can be gifts.

The truth of it is, despite the statistics about alienation and hedonic treadmills, there is a rumbling revolution, a counter-current of many people like Greg looking for more.

A friend at Google pulled me in to do a project for them, and I got to see the "Google way" up close. The folks there are practically on tiptoe with excitement about the things they can do to make the world better: digitizing Oxford University's library so that a kid in say, Senegal, can read any book there, or linking translated news stories in 117 languages so that anyone, anywhere, can know what people are saying in other parts of the world. Their business philosophy is full of idealism, the much-vaunted (and parodied) slogan "Don't be evil" key among its tenets.

The Google folks are explicitly out to build a new model that forgoes short-term gain for long-term good and that serves other people in addition to their shareholders.[35] Google and quite a few other new-economy companies have left modernity. They are living the next thing. In Google, you can do good while doing well, and there aren't many recipes for success (and happiness) better than that.

The happy truth is that there are thousands of Americans, in all walks of life and business, who are putting tremendous effort into making a difference. Why aren't a thousand threads good enough? Because nothing can beat the good that comes from knitting individual effort together with great group effort.

Frank

Kathy speaks of doing good while doing well. I don't think it's a coincidence that Kathy's altruistic friend had a Roman Catholic mother. But the question is this: what will Kathy's friend pass on to his children if he is operating on the mere memory of someone else's spiritual commitment? To do good you have to define what good is. And to do that you have to ask yourself a question: what is authentic purpose?

I first saw it in my father—when he was being himself, that is, and not playing the role of proselytizer. Dad set an example by authentically loving ideas. And he showed me how a life informed by aesthetic appreciation may be achieved or at least struggled for. The point was this: if you find the world beautiful and discover value in what people create, it will motivate you to help all people and nurture our earth. For Dad, that came close to the definition of holiness.

I think the "it" of my dad's life was found in that clear bell-like note we hear when we encounter the real and the lasting in others and in ourselves. The even bigger trick is something akin to seeing in the dark. It's like adjusting our inner vision by deliberately *not* looking into bright lights of false certainties, so that we can see life through eyes accustomed to subtler shades.

Kathy

We have our brave new pioneers already for this new era, men and women living free, bringing themselves and their talents to the world, building something new, contributing as they go, full of optimism. What we lack is a national purpose to bind them together and to give anchor to their energies. Consequently, the talent is giving up on the public sphere. The old guard and the new are shrugging and walking away.

Turning to private sources of solutions to our problems—

private philanthropy, private nonprofits, private enterprise—is fine. There is nothing wrong with private effort. But when not tethered to the agora, private initiatives ultimately are not democratic. There's a place for the wholly private, but there's a more important place for the truly public.

Sure, we could use leaders to articulate a common good, a space race, a Manifest Destiny to bind us; a sustainable world, perhaps. But we need something even more than a great leader. We need great people.

Frank

People can't be greater than their ideas about themselves. What we need to do first is change our ideas. To do that we have to repudiate the personal and national philosophy of life that is making us unhappy *and* destroying our earth's ability to sustain life.

That means saying goodbye and good riddance to defining ourselves as consumers. That means affirming a higher vision of life than a merely material one. That means no longer defining freedom as the "right" to choose between products. That means believing that our individual rights should be defined by a commitment to others.

14. Politics Matters

Kathy

In 1987 I was holed up in a little windowless back room of a former car showroom in Des Moines, Iowa, four blocks from the state capitol. I had a very bad perm, there was way too much fluorescent lighting in my office, and my walls were plastered with poster board scrawled with schedules and maps of different regions. I was twenty-three years old and working for Paul Simon's presidential campaign. Life was great.

Pretty soon, the temperature would be dropping to thirty degrees below zero with the windchill factor. The morning radio announcers would remind us cheerfully, "Flesh freezes in fifteen minutes in this weather, so wear your gloves!" I lived in an apartment building with the rest of the campaign staff and logged a hundred hours of work per week. And all that just made it better.

The only people with the time, energy, and willingness to take on the ridiculously low pay (sometimes no pay) of primary work, at least in those days, were kids like me. Our old man was the thirty-year-old state campaign manager, Pat Mitchell, a lawyer on leave. Our field staff was even younger than me. Andy Cowan and Max Stier were earnest, smart guys just out of Yale, working to win their corner of the state from their padded orange cubicles. Rob Johnson was our gonzo advance director, famous for things like getting a police escort back to Des Moines at 90 mph after convincing the cop who pulled him over that he worked for the Bush campaign. Soon Ed Emerson would join us, with his stories of holding Hunter S. Thompson in a headlock in a bar fight. And Mike Lux was the "local genius," twenty-seven years old, shuffling around in no tie and old chinos, whether the candidate was there or not.

We poached Lux from the Biden campaign after Biden flamed out with a speech about how he grew up around the coal mines playing football. It turned out the speech and the memories belonged to British Labour party candidate Neil Kinnock—oops. Poaching top staff from the Biden campaign was one of our major intrigues. In the competition for Biden's staff we beat the evil IBM-style Dukakis campaign juggernaut, run by Iowa mastermind Teresa Vilmain (who is not evil, though she does reincarnate every four years, most recently as Hillary Clinton's Iowa director). Needless to say, we all eventually went to work for Dukakis in the general election, but hey, this was the primaries.

We were comrades in aims, united in our cause. We went drinking together at the biker bar across the road, Pat and Mike's. We kept an office cat. These were the days before AIDS scares and sexual harassment laws, and there were a lot more men then women, so it was a buyer's market for we few women as far as dating went. We hung out with the Pulitzer Prize–winning, cigar-smoking national reporters, who had been exiled to Iowa because of the unusually long primary season, at places like Taste of Thailand, which was dubbed the "foreign press club of Des Moines" and boasted a beer garden with 113 different varieties.

The luckiest thing about the whole episode, for me, was our candidate, Senator Paul Simon. Not everyone remembers him. He retired in 1996 and died too young at age seventy-five in 2003. He wore a bow tie all the time, and thick glasses. He wouldn't have won any beauty contests. But what a guy, and what a great man for me to have run into early in my years in politics.

Paul Simon went into politics for all the right reasons and stayed there his entire life, deep into it to the tips of his enormous ears, without getting rich or changing the suits he wore or his hometown. In the end he left for the right reasons: because he was spending too much time fund-raising, and because he wanted to spend more of what time he had left with his wife, Jeanne. In the end, they packed their unswanky apartment furniture into a U-Haul truck and drove home to Makanda, Illinois, population 401.

I toured him around the White House once, years later when I was a staffer. He marveled at the history of the storied rooms, and he thanked me sincerely, without seeming to register that he could have requested the visit through his office as a perk. I didn't know the young Paul Simon, but I knew the stories. He dropped out of college when the only newspaper in his town folded, took out a loan to buy the paper, and became the country's youngest publisher-editor at age nineteen, running a series of muckraking stories exposing government corruption. He did a stint in the Army during the Korean War, then spent most of the rest of his life doing his best to do what's right as a guy elected to serve.

There may not be bucketloads of saints like Paul Simon in politics, but one saint is perhaps enough to keep one's faith in the system strong. And the truth is, most people I know in politics are there because they want to do the right thing.

I get disgusted and turned off, just like everyone else, by the lobbying, the money, and the pork barrel projects. There's way too much self-interest in politics, and a soul-crushing amount of fund-raising. But at heart it is an exciting, even thrilling proposition that we can govern ourselves, that our future is in our hands.

Frank

What can get us all into the associations Kathy advocates? What might be big enough to motivate the bitterest bloggers from the left and the right to say something nice about each other for once? It won't be happening at some conference or symposium with the slogan "Can't we all just get along?" It will happen only if believers and nonbelievers can agree on one big thing.

This can't be some wishy-washy "middle way" or (God forbid) a sappy new-speak Clintonesque "third way." This will work only if everyone *actually becomes convinced that our survival truly depends on each other.*

Kathy and I believe that human beings function best with a sense of purpose. But there's a difference between us when it comes to our ideas about why we humans do certain things or how to motivate certain good behaviors. I naturally draw on my deepest beliefs to define what I mean by the words "good behaviors," whereas I think Kathy throws around the terms *good* and *bad* rather loosely. Who will define what those terms mean?

Kathy

We've done it before, and we can do it again. Our ability to work together beyond our narrow self-interest shaped us as a country. The British peer James Bryce wrote in the 1890s, sixty years after Tocqueville, about volunteer groups that threw a network across the continent, taking on "great importance in the development of opinion . . . they rouse attention, excite discussion, formulate principles, submit plans, embolden and stimulate their members."[36]

Even as our country was re-forming in the twentieth century for the new, consumer era, everyday people continued to organize. Operating very much in republican mode, people created large voluntary organizations that drew the bulk of Americans into the business of participating in the running of their country, or at least into having the feeling that they were participating and therefore developing a sense of connection and empowerment.

At that time, the AFL-CIO counted 12 percent of the population among its membership. The American Legion sponsored the signature legislation of the middle of the twentieth century, the single bit of legislation that perhaps did the most toward leveling the playing field in America and ensuring future prosperity: the GI Bill. This gave the men and women who fought for their country the ability to go to college. And with that innovation we became the most educated nation in the world, at least in terms of the percentage of our people who attended college.

These organizations weren't lobbying groups as we know them today. These groups *actually met*. The participants took part, learned the skills of senators, held debates, and suggested bills; there were no paid staffs, no hired administrators, professional researchers, or insider lobbyists. The members did the work themselves.

Today we have a staggeringly large number of associations and groups, but the difference is that they are almost all top-down. They did not have to test their appeal by recruiting local chapters, holding their members' interest. Increasingly today, "members" are members in name only. Their only activity is to write a check, or maybe to send or read a group e-mail or blogs. Professional staff lobby for their association's interest. According to Harvard sociologist Theda Skocpol, an expert on volunteer groups and their disappearance in America, "The universe of very large American membership associations today is much less concerned with brotherhood, sisterhood, fellow citizenship, and community service than ever before in the nation's long history."[37]

Many of the most powerful American groups before the last third of the twentieth century were built on the idea of patriotism and the idea that we all have a stake in our country. But, as George Plimpton put it, sometime in the late sixties intellectualism and patriotism went their separate ways, to the detriment of both.

Patriotism fell out of favor because it was thought to be at odds with the self-expression of the modern era: consumers choose things, and so they shouldn't have obligations thrust on them. Only people's rights mattered. The state was the entity that threatened to usurp individuals' rights.

In the pre–Vietnam War days military service accentuated civic and economic equality. The head of the New York Stock Exchange served. Presidents' sons served. The scion of the publisher of the *New York Times* did too, as did celebrities Joe DiMaggio and Clark Gable. And so veterans were central to all of the major voluntary organizations in America. People met different sorts of Americans, bonded with them through service, and came home to a grateful nation.

Today, military service is asked of only about 5 percent of the population, and it is increasingly drawing from a narrow slice of American society: the middle and lower middle classes primarily from military families in the South and Midwest. Consequently, service no longer has the broadening and deepening effect it once had. In that sense we've lost something from the post-Vietnam, all-volunteer military, regardless of its ability to project power. It no longer contributes to the civic melting-pot effect the way it used to. The eclipse of national patriotism "dissolved much of the moral glue that enabled cross-class associations to flourish."[38]

Those who fought in our wars once exemplified cross-class brotherhood. However, after Vietnam, national solidarity and patriotism became suspect, especially among the educated elites, affected as they were by a generalized postmodern cynicism that will forgive just about anything except earnestness. Cynicism isn't all bad—it's a continuation of the shift of power from figureheads to the people. But cynicism and distrust are only productive if they are twinned with the energy to create and contribute to something better. Class distinctions are more powerful in our country today than in any time since the Gilded Age, the age of the robber barons. Rich people's money and influence go where the privileged folks choose, to circles they know. And since there is no draft, there is no time in their lives when the privileged are forced (or even encouraged) to mingle with Americans of all classes.

Today, Americans socialize within their class, and by and large only with people who agree with them about politics, social issues, or religion. Ambitious, educated, and moneyed people don't need to bother mobilizing the masses as they did through the mid-twentieth century to secure power and influence. Their freedom to travel means they are no longer restricted to social groups based in their hometowns. Today's educated elite probably have friends of different races and religions, but not of different classes, and often not with different ideas.

Today, all of our de facto schools for citizenship are in decline. The falloff in club meetings, visits with friends, committee service, certain denominations' church attendance (not all church attendance is down; the evangelicals are flourishing), gifts to charity, card games, and electoral turnout have hit virtually all sectors of American society. This is equally true for women and men, the coasts and the heartland, renters and homeowners, small towns and urban centers, rich and poor, married and unmarried, Republicans and Democrats, parents and childless.[39]

We have less of the glue that makes us feel connected to the enterprise of being America. We're not going to go back. Military service will never be the melting pot it was. Something else will have to take its place. We need schools for citizenship, schools for "senators," to train us, change us, so that we can be up to the challenges that face us.

15. Principles Matter

Frank

What specific community will pressure the rest of us into wanting their approval and therefore changing our consumerist behavior? To put it several other ways: How will communism in China fare now that the communists aren't communists anymore? How well has the American Jewish community done at retaining its Jewish identity after so many American Jews decided to become atheists? How long will the freedoms we take for granted in the West remain after the disappearance of the Christian religion that spawned the principles expressed in the Magna Carta, English common law, and the insights of the Enlightenment?

Kathy

Frank has a point. The modern developed countries are the first in the world to remove ideas of faith and morality from the public places where people are supposed to talk about how to run their societies. There are many people who will read that sentence and say, "Good for us!" There are many others who will read it and shake their heads.

I think this removal of talk of faith and morality from the public sphere is good and bad. It's good because it removes the exclusionary and bigoted side of religion. It's bad because we may need ideas of transcendent purpose to move us to engage in the greater good.

The language of values left the public space because of the one-two punch of shopping and law. If consumerism is what matters, then what people want (to choose) matters, and since everyone doesn't buy in to the same virtues, it's best to just take 'em out of the places people meet.

As we've decided that it's not the government's job to help form citizens' moral character, we've chosen rights over ideas of good. Choosing which values are good seems to get in the way of individual liberty. So it's believed by many that it's better not to mention it. And this legalistic focus on rights (which developed in the last half of the twentieth century) has meant that government and the law has become more and more concerned with the process of public decisions. The process now trumps the content.

The sad thing is that we've impoverished ourselves by

taking the language of meaning out of the public square. We've left churches, temples, and mosques as some of the few places where people can hear about transcendent purpose and character virtues. The problem with this is that it's the public square, not the houses of worship, where we are all unified. We've got to stop beggaring the common square of meaning if we want to make it a compelling place to be, if we want to forge bonds between ourselves that are strong enough to reinvigorate our republic.

It turns out that mere rational theory can't get us to shared purpose. In the end, you don't eat your vegetables because they're good for you; you eat your vegetables because they taste good. And the language of values is what makes common purpose appealing.

It is in our self-interest to develop our character. But only the soaring language of the spirit will motivate and inspire. So next comes the tricky part. If we need to restore values in the public sphere again, whose values should they be? Where will they come from?

Frank

We can't deal with life's big moments in purely rational terms, let alone strictly legalistic ones. "Soaring language"? What tradition does the soaring language plug into?

When my son John was at war he experienced bleak moments. It's interesting that in his most brutally honest letter home (from the war in Afghanistan, sent as an e-mail during his first deployment), when trying to express something about the horror of warfare, John resorted to the moral and inherently religious vocabulary rooted in our Greek Orthodox liturgical rituals.

Date: 9/25/03 8:27:01 P.M. Eastern Daylight Time
From: John Schaeffer
To: Mom and Dad

Dear Mom and Dad: I have learned that the right thing and the necessary thing are not synonymous, rarely are they even in the same ballpark. . . . There is no purity here. I have started to pray again.

I have realized that without faith there is no hope. I also realize why many Americans and people of privilege everywhere do not pray. But there are some places where faith is the only thing that can make you take the next step. It is the only hope. It is not a choice. It is all there is.

When I come home, I'll be lighting about 200 candles. . . .

When we get to the basics of love, life, death, and war, what vocabulary is there that can capture our deepest feelings besides the vocabulary of spirituality? John's reference to lighting those candles was about repentance. (Within the Greek Orthodox religious tradition, prayer is symbolized by lighting candles.) The Orthodox Church teaches that war may sometimes be necessary, but it's always a tragedy nonetheless. (The appreciation of paradox is alive and well within the Orthodox tradition.) John wanted to light those candles even though he believed in what he was doing in Afghanistan. He still needed a spiritual way to come to terms with war.

Kathy

There are virtues that are good for societies, and virtues that are good for people—the character traits Frank talks about. The virtues on these lists are pretty much the same ones written on the squadron stairs at the military base I lived on. No one says you have to believe in God to like that list. So we don't have to answer the question Frank asks, about where those traits come from. They are ours—isn't that good enough?

Frank

No. But I'll meet Kathy halfway: I don't think we need to be religious to act morally as individuals. Some of the most upright and trustworthy people I know are dogmatically secular—for instance, my best and very old friend, entertainment attorney and columnist Frank Gruber, who is a Jewish agnostic, and Frank's atheist philosophy professor wife, Janet. And some of the most awful people I've ever met are the most religious. But that doesn't change the fact that "values" just become niceties without an overarching belief system for which you are willing to sacrifice.

Kathy

So I'm confused, Frank. Do the Grubers have an overarching belief system?

Frank

Yes. They have a Jewish-agnostic-atheist-ethical system that is no less principled than any religious believer's faith.

Kathy

Frank! You surprise me!

Frank

I would bet anything that the Grubers would sacrifice ease, well-being, even life for their principles. I'd trust an ethically motivated atheist or agnostic over a believing Christian who lived less consistently with his or her principles.

I think that Frank Gruber articulated Kathy's view when he e-mailed me this:

I believe in law, specifically in the Constitution of the United States. I have no problem agreeing that without the Judeo-

Christian tradition, there would be no Constitution, no Bill
of Rights, no Fourteenth Amendment, but once written and
adopted, these laws must be interpreted on their own terms.
There is no "natural law" to turn to, no "natural rights"
that supersede the rights we have under law.

Is everything that neat and tidy? Have we passed through a religious era into another, more rational one—thanks for the memories, we'll take it from here, game over?

I'm not so sure. My father believed that if the idea of biblical, God-given absolutes was abandoned by the West, there would be a real question as to where any new morality would come from. This is a question that secular writers such as Robert Wright have also examined and drawn similar conclusions about, for very different reasons, and which I don't think my friend Frank answered.

Dad used to hold forth on issues of inconsistency, such as the hippie movement's inability to realize its idealistic promise or to provide a lasting alternative social model. "While their analysis of the bankruptcy of our plastic society is right, they have no answer," Dad would say, and add prophetically: "You wait—the hippies are going to wind up more middle-class, bourgeois, and materialistic than their parents, only with even less principles."

Dad's predictions were fulfilled in the life and times of Walter Bowart, someone whose life is symbolic of a whole generation, almost to the point of parody. A *New York Times* obituary described Bowart as the "founder and the first publisher of *The East Village Other*, a New York newspaper so countercultural that it made *The Village Voice* look like a church circular."

Published from 1965 to 1972, *The East Village Other* was among the country's first major underground newspapers. "For seven heady years, *The East Village Other* waxed lyrical on the counterculture's movers and shakers, among them Timothy Leary and Abbie Hoffman. As publisher, Mr. Bowart came to national attention in 1966 after he recommended, in testimony before the Senate Subcommittee on Juvenile Delinquency, that the committee members try LSD."

How did Mr. Bowart's revolutionary life work out on the ideological front? The *Times* describes where he ended up: "In the late 1980s he was the editor of *Palm Springs Life* magazine, which, according to recent promotional materials, covers 'celebrities, luxury homes, fine art and dining, fashion, golf and society.'"

Dad would often say, "The hippies will soon be about nothing but personal peace and affluence at any price. They'll follow anyone who will promise that." Dad died in 1984, but he more or less predicted the Ginsburg-to-golf-and-fine-dining Bowarts of this world, not to mention President Bush's reaction to 9/11, a reaction that had to invent a "bad guy" (Saddam Hussein) to be attacked for something he hadn't done. Dad would have said the Iraq War, not to mention the Bush administration's use of torture (by whatever name), was a way of lashing out, driven by fears that "they" would interrupt our consumer lifestyle.

I guess the basic difference between us is that Kathy believes that the rule of law, dressed up with a little values-speak to "inspire," is sufficient in itself to provide us with general principles. I think that the rule of law has to be founded on some higher aspiration in order to give it an aura that will survive self-interest and fear. In that sense there's something to be said for the so-called Calvinist work ethic, just as there is a lot to be said for the idea of God-is-watching-me moral rectitude that post-Reformation northern European countries lived by for so long (before they went secular in the twentieth century en masse). In those countries the idea of corruption in government is still generally unthinkable.

There are lots of cultures that—on paper—have founding documents as impressive as ours. What they lack is the cultural and religious character formation to uphold and actually put into practice the things they say they believe.

When Japanese Americans were getting locked up during World War II or when the CIA tortures Islamic terrorist suspects today, someone needs to be able to say "This is wrong" and give that statement more weight than a simple "I think" or "the law says." Without an ultimate moral purpose somewhere in the argument, why should people care? "Says who?" is the logical rejoinder to calls to do the "right thing" when doing what's right will cost us. What is the comeback to "But this works!" or, worse, "We all voted for this" when it comes to torturing prisoners if that is proven to make us secure?

Moral action depends on a willingness to sacrifice—for instance, a willingness to sacrifice some national security for a higher principle. To do that, you have to know who you are. To know who you are, you have to know what you believe. And if all you believe in is legal process, rather than in the ideas that give the rule of law meaning—for instance, in the idea that because of sin we need checks on our behavior—will your system be able to face real challenges when it will cost you to do the right thing?

Kathy has linked happiness science to our thesis as if that answers everything, as in "If it feels good, do it." But what happens when what needs to be done feels bad?

For instance, I think that to stop the slide toward environmental degradation we'll need to sacrifice certain things about our standard of living. It's going to hurt. I think that in order to remain who we Americans say we are, we'll need to sacrifice a certain measure of security rather than allow our civil rights to erode. Some people may die as a result.

Kathy

Frank tosses off "the rule of law" as though it's a little thing. In fact, it's an amazing triumph of human potential. Prior to the rule of law, the only way to resolve disputes (such as what religion should we follow, or where's the border of this land) was force or fear. The legal process supplants that, says there is a basis for accepting decisions separate from force or the self-interest of those in power. Sure, laws are skewed toward the powerful, but those with less power win too. There's a long history of law; it wasn't invented by Christians, and it isn't exclusive to them. It's human. And the things we are able to do—exchange power peacefully, lose our emotional and religious battles peacefully, these are all due to the rule of law.

Frank

Kathy misunderstands me. To put it differently: I'm talking about having a moral compass that gives the rule of law meaning. The issue is, how do you behave when nobody's watching? What's the difference between society's rules and the ones you carry around inside you?

Kathy

Frank doesn't know what it's like to live comfortably and ethically in a secular world. I've lived both sides of the secular-faith divide in the middle-of-the-road way common to most people, not on the extremes where Frank has walked, so I speak about this a bit from the inside. As I mentioned before, I was raised secular and ethical, in a manner familiar to educated suburbanites across America. I didn't really believe in God, or a locus of transcendent morality, until I was thirty-eight years old, which, as I write, was about five years ago. But I did believe in trying to do good, I believed in the idea of life having meaning.

People raised as I was learn that humans had lots of superstitions and misconceptions about the world as we evolved, from the notion that the sun revolved around the earth to the idea that you could heal a sick person by bleeding. The notion of God, in this construct, is simply one of many outmoded ideas. God was the mother of all superstitions. Those raised as Christians may learn about Jesus as a self-correcting influence, as Frank says, but Jews can't help noticing that it took about two thousand years for the self-correction to kick in as far as disenfranchising and killing Jews went.

God couldn't be proved by science, so that was the end of it. As for the fact that people continue to believe in God today, my father had an explanation: it had to do with neurosis and psychological needs. The implication was that healthy people are not religious.

I grew up assuming that most people no longer believed in God. They might go to church or temple for social reasons, but actual belief in God had gone the way of the horse and buggy.

I didn't really understand until I got to high school that not all Christians liked each other. I did get involved in a youth group at a local church at one point, mostly because a good friend of mine invited me, and because they organized a lot of fun "good works," such as visiting old-age homes and repairing rural schools. The other kids and the youth leader were unfazed by me being nominally Jewish, and their theology seemed to be summed up in a facile phrase some of them liked: "God loves you and I do too." (And let's be fair—the older kids in the group indulged in drugs and sex, too; it wasn't all sweet good works.)

I wasn't raised with the Ten Commandments, but I was raised to be moral, to try to make a difference in the world. I thought that when you died, that was it; you turned to dust. That didn't lessen the need to do good while you were alive, and it didn't prevent inspiration or hope. When you were dead, well, you'd have no consciousness, so it didn't really matter.

The slog through the years of my parents' divorce and their struggles to rebuild their lives was hard. Sometimes I leaned on the faith that the troubles were transient. My troubles didn't last as long as the trees, for instance. I leaned on the simple and obvious beauty at our fingertips—yellow butterflies on green leaves, that sort of thing. That was a secular faith for me, not one I connected to an idea of God. And my parents did slowly rebuild their lives. I heard about that as it happened. My mom would come into my room after I went to bed, sit on the edge of my bed in the dark, and talk. Sometimes we'd talk for hours.

This kind of faith is almost physical. It leans on physical truth, and on beauty, as Frank talked about related to art, which can have its own transcendent meaning. These were lessons that made me feel smaller, less important, but not in a bad way; rather, it was in a way that made the hard times seem smaller and less important too. And we all eventually got better over time. My mother brightened and found new legs in the world. I launched myself on adventures.

Ten years after my parents' bitter divorce, in 1986, I was with my friends Susie and Claudia in the basement of our dorm at Bryn Mawr College. It was about eleven at night, and we were laughing and chatting as we returned from a night out, heading into the laundry room with our quarters to work the dryers. Lisa Brody was just walking out; she was from my town, and her dad had gone to high school with my mom. Her face was flushed, and she looked surprised to see me. And the first thing she asked was very odd: "Kathy, was your mom in Mexico?"

"Yes, she went on holiday with her boyfriend."

Lisa hesitated.

"I got a phone call from my parents. There's been something on the radio. A plane crash. They didn't think there were any survivors." She started crying. "I'm so sorry."

I remember Susie and Claudia holding on to me from either side. I felt as though an abyss had just opened at my feet, that if I lost my balance I'd tumble in and fall and fall and fall forever into the blackness.

Children love mothers, but the circumstances of our lives—the match of our personalities and the closeness that sutures single mothers and daughters together—had made my mother and me intimate. She was in my corner no matter what; her arms were always open for me; she could listen to me for hours (who else would ever do that?) . . . and she was gone. Gone without goodbyes.

I met something that neither mental gymnastics or activism or even the yellow butterfly on the green leaf could make better. My mother was gone, and she wasn't coming back. This proved that anyone could be gone at any moment. Life is fragile. We are terribly vulnerable. Loss walks with us.

In the later months of mourning I was continually astonished at the extraordinary fact of death. The most intractable truth was this: death was an unimaginable tragedy to me, the loss unremitting, and yet it was banal, quotidian. It was the one thing that happened to every single person, and no one could avoid enduring it. How could something be unbearable yet mundane? And this is when I began to realize what a wonderful thing it would be to believe in God.

If belief in God could hold the terrible sense of anomie at bay, keep away the icy fear of being an insignificant atom lost, alone, in space, then it would be a great thing to have. But you can't switch on belief, just as you can't force yourself to fall in love at first sight.

The rational life has no answer for anomie. It is either indifferent to the problem or defenseless in the face of it. I tried to attack that scary nothingness by weaving myself into a web of life, of connections to other people, of friendships and far-flung family, of activities and work, all of them lassoes to hold me down, keep at bay the terrible risk of drifting away.

Community helps, work with purpose helps, but it can't keep you busy all the time. Fear slips in at night, at odd times. And the more you have in your life that you love, the more you have to lose.

Eventually I won the life lottery. I married happily and soon had two mind-bogglingly wonderful children. When they were little, sometimes I would wake up at night. I would feel how fast the last ten years had gone by, know it was only a matter of moments before decades more would slip through my hands and all this joy, all this perfection would be gone. I would grow old, they would grow old, unforeseen accidents would befall us.

I could so easily see my own speeding end and the inevitability of having to leave Greg and the kids. I also experienced the freezing black thought that they would leave me first and I would be utterly bereft. I would feel helpless at the sadness of it all and amazed that the whole world's population, all of whom face these same problems, is somehow able to set that sadness aside. I wasn't gripped by this sense of unavoidable tragedy often, but it came often enough for it to be dreadful.

The only way to address it that I could think of was to try to believe in God. But how?

Judaism, a religion centered very much on practice, has a response to this problem. If you want to believe in God but you don't, you should *act* like you believe in God. This is one of the ways Judaism differs from Christianity. Often Christians say you have to believe first, then change will follow. Judaism says act first, and belief will follow.

It sounds kooky, but this is what I did. I acted as I thought I would act if I believed in God. I sent my daughter to Jewish preschool, and I taught her to believe in God. I talked to her as though I did believe in God, explaining things, explaining morality in a way that included God. I prepared Friday night dinners, thought about the ideas of making the profane holy, read and thought about other religious ideas. Not to overstate it: I didn't spend a great deal of time on it, and I only sporadically attended synagogue, in part because my husband is Christian and I didn't want to divide up our family time, in part because I'm kind of lazy.

In the end, my daughter and my husband took me to a more concrete faith. In 2003 my husband was with the invading forces that entered Iraq. You can imagine how excruciating it is for someone as finely attuned to the potential for loss as I am to endure the fact of my husband being in so much danger. I needed something to help me cope, and I'm not disposed to alcohol or drugs (and sex would be pretty tacky under the circumstances).

Then one day in April 2003 (before Baghdad fell) I was talking to my four-year-old in our living room, explaining that you should be kind to someone's annoying little sister because that's what God wants you to do. As I was saying that, I was thinking of how I would explain that same lesson without God.

Where do rules about kindness come from? And simply saying "just because" or "because I said so" didn't seem good enough to back it up. I would have had to construct some convoluted narrative about neurophysiology, genetics, and anthropology that sidesteps most of history (after all, *unkindness* to strangers is also explainable by neurophysiology, genetics, and anthropology) to somehow come up with an explanation for why some moral behavior is correct. Or I'd be trying to appeal to her selfish interest, explaining other people as an instrument to get what you want, so if you're kind, you're more likely to get kindness back. (But what if she doesn't care about the little sister being kind to her in the future?) Instead of saying that other people are really whole and important in themselves, I'd actually be rationalizing excuses for bad behavior.

And suddenly it seemed that, in fact, the idea that there is a *source* of morality, a source separate from human genes and their programming, seemed much simpler, more elegant, and ultimately more convincingly true than the other explanations.

Something about my daughter's instant, sure, and intuitive grasp of the idea of transcendent morality, and my need in the face of the war, made the whole conundrum of belief slip into my hands with the sudden completeness of a Rubik's Cube in its final stage, the sides becoming solid colors with a single last click. I felt the dilation of the chest, the expansion and slight elation that believers report in the apprehension of God.

It has stayed with me since. Not always, but when I need it, it is a wonderful thing. What does it mean?

At heart, my idea of faith is the notion that there is a mystery larger than men and women, not knowable to us but benign. It is the source of what is moral and right, and of what is best about us. Moreover, it is a mystery we do not have to solve. That means that I do not have to know the other side of unknowables that frighten me, like the death of people I love. I can take it on faith that mysteries can remain mysteries in the domain of a goodness that exists separate from me. It's kind of like Frank's "thus sayeth the Lord," but maybe with one or two more steps of abstraction.

A sense of that larger goodness is a source of connection to other people, and a source of inspiration and motivation. I have experienced nothing bad about believing in God (or transcendent morality, if the word *God* makes you uncomfortable). It has given me a stronger faith that everything will be all right and a sense of relief that it doesn't all depend on me. This sense of transcendent faith has kept the abyss at bay and can be a source of happiness. It's a gift I'm happy to accept.

But am I a better person, or a different person, than I would have been if the circumstance of my life hadn't led me to chase down a connection to God? I don't think so.

Of course, those who behave badly sometimes turn around

with a religious conversion, as did the slave-trading author of the hymn "Amazing Grace." But those people whose behavior is good, or good enough, don't need to turn around. Trying to be a good person isn't predicated on believing in God. That's not an argument for or against religion. It's an argument for common ground.

16. God and Darwin Shake Hands

Frank

I agree. And Kathy's point is worth repeating: "Trying to be a good person isn't predicated on believing in God. That's not an argument for or against religion. It's an argument for common ground."

For those of us who believe in God, the argument to work together with people who don't believe, in order to preserve our planet and our democracy, is simple: we are to be good stewards. For those of us who don't believe in God, the argument to work together with people who do believe, in order to preserve our planet and our democracy, is also simple: we live here.

Psychologist David Myers says that people who believe in God function better.[40] Kathy tells me that the founder of positive psychology, Martin Seligman, says that religion is a "top predictor" of happiness.[41] That means that religious people are either right to believe or just lucky in the delusion we are consumed by.

Dead white Christian (and Jewish) males didn't invent or impose human nature. Nature and/or God did. Living within and admitting that truth is one route to happiness. As Kathy says, happiness science finds that for well-being we need to cultivate internal qualities of character and external ties that bring meaning to our lives. This contemporary science is in hearty agreement with centuries of philosophy and the signature religious insights. It also seems to echo some of the psychological and genetic studies that Wright examines.

> But if evolutionary psychology is on track, the whole picture [of how we see ourselves and therefore pursue our ideas of happiness] needs to be turned inside out. We believe the things—about morality, personal worth, even objective truth—that lead to behaviors that get our genes into the next generation. (Or at least we believe the kinds of things that, in the environment of our evolution, would have been likely to get our genes into the next generation.) It is the behavioral goals—status, sex, effective coalition, parental investment, and so on—that remain steadfast while our view of reality adjusts to accommodate this constancy. What is in our genes' interest is what seems "right"—morally right, objectively right, whatever sort of rightness is in order.[42]

Secularism has failed to replace religion. Too bad. It would have been nice to move on to some higher plain.

Believe it or not, I hate writing about religion. I can't wait to get my part of this book off my chest—help Kathy save the world—and then get back to any subject (say, writing my next novel) that gets me off the radar screen of some very odd folks.

After my memoir *Crazy for God* was published in 2007, I was quickly reminded of why I'd left the evangelical world. I got literally hundreds of terrific, kind, smart, and interesting e-mails from evangelicals and/or former evangelicals. But I also received a flood of semi-rational messages and blog comments from people offering to punch me in the mouth, on one hand, and/or begging me to embrace the love of Jesus, on the other, sometimes in the *same* e-mail or blog. An amazing number of those comments began with, "I've not read the book but . . ." and then immediately went into a theological or ad hominem tirade.

That said, religion is something we have to face. Does anyone sincerely think that we're *not* entering the next age of religion? From the religiously earnest pages of left-wing secular blogs to Islam to emerging Pentecostal movements in Asia and Africa (and perhaps even a new Christian majority someday emerging in China), from evangelicals in North America to modern Turkey turning rightward and Islamic to renewed Hindu fervor in India—the fight is over: humankind is religious. So let's reframe the argument.

Maybe we can embrace our shared human heritage that leads us to care about character strength and virtue, that leads us to value intangibles like hope and love over and above our diverse theologies. In any case, we have to go beyond our previous societies, beyond self-sufficiency, beyond self-expression, beyond consuming, beyond a sense that "I am my rights" and beyond religion—including mine.

Kathy

Judaism has no original sin, no sacrifice (it has gradually been removed from practice), and so it is not about redemption. It is about this world and acting in accordance with the right way, for no ultimate reward other than doing the right thing right here and now. It's not a proselytizing religion—other nations belong to God too, and they do not need to convert to live a good life.

That said, though I call myself Jewish, I'm by no means a traditional Jew. And I'm not moving Frank's way either. I don't believe that Jesus was divine. On the other hand, I don't deny it. If he was, I'll find out soon enough.

I think there are truths in many religions, and we can all use wisdom however we can get it. This makes me more New Age in my belief. But maybe Frank and I are a good pair to talk about this. Maybe each of us can find our group of people who is more willing to listen to us because our views more closely match theirs.

Frank

Here is a religious statement of a reason to protect our earth and human ecology. In his book *Pollution and the Death of Man* my father wrote:

> *If things are treated only as machines in a de-created world they are finally meaningless. But if that is so, then inevitably so am I—man—also equally meaningless. But if individually and in the Christian community, I treat the things which God has made with integrity and treat them this way lovingly, because they are His, things change.*
>
> *If I love the Lover, I love what the Lover has made. Perhaps this is the reason why so many Christians feel the unreality in their Christian lives. If I don't love what the Lover has made—in the area of nature—and really love it because He made it, do I really love the Lover? I must be clear that I am not loving the tree or whatever is standing in front of me, for a pragmatic reason. It will have a pragmatic result, the very pragmatic result that the men involved in ecology are looking for. But as a Christian I do not do it for the practical or pragmatic results: I do it because it is right and because God is the maker.*[43]

Here is a secular statement of the same principle. David Myers writes from a less specifically theological position but comes to the same conclusion.

So we face that fork in the road. We have, as Solzhenitsyn said in concluding his commencement address at Harvard, "reached a major watershed in history, equal in importance to the turn from the Middle Ages to the Renaissance. It will demand from us a spiritual blaze: we shall have to rise to a new height of vision, a new level of life, where our physical nature will not be cursed, as in the Middle Ages, but even more importantly, our spiritual being will not be trampled upon, as in the Modern Era."

This ascension is similar to climbing to the next anthropological stage. No one on earth has any other way left—but upward.[44]

Kathy and I think that there is little to disagree with in either of the statements above. Even the zealous atheist Richard Dawkins, in his famous book *The Selfish Gene*, makes a dispassionate scientific observation that may not have the spiritual fervor of the statements above but nevertheless seems to come to the same conclusion, in terms of human strategies of cooperation that are in line with what he would regard as our gene-driven behavior.

An evolutionarily stable strategy or ESS is defined as a strategy which, if most members of a population adopt it, cannot be bettered by an alternative strategy. It is a subtle and important idea. Another way of putting it is to say that the best strategy for an individual depends on what the majority of the population are doing. Since the rest of the population consists of individuals, each one trying to maximize his own success, the only strategy that persists will be one which, once evolved, cannot be bettered by any deviant individual. . . .

I have a hunch that we may come to look back on the invention of the ESS concept as one of the most important advances in evolutionary theory since Darwin. . . . I think this will be true not only of social organizations within species, but also of "ecosystems" and "communities" consisting of many species. In the long term, I expect the ESS concept to revolutionize the science of ecology.[45]

In other words, the sort of cooperation and care that people like my father called for from a religious basis and that Myers calls for from a general spiritual (and utilitarian and pragmatic) point of view is, according to Dawkins, mirrored in the concept of ESS in nature. Again, this is where the material world and religions intersect. This is what we can *all* agree on.

Fulfilling a new vision of ourselves that is matched by real change in what we do, and therefore who we become, will require moral purpose and actual belief in a higher call of some kind, even if that only means we admit that our genes make us act in certain ways and make us feel happy when we are altruistic.

We're on a small blue planet, and we threaten to overwhelm it. What is our moral purpose? To live as if God exists and cares about the earth He made and the humans on it. What is our moral purpose? To live as if God doesn't exist and this life is all we have.

Kathy

Here's something else we all have in common: we are *all* naive realists. That means, in psychological terms, that all people are biased by their past experiences and particular world-views. We know that in everybody's case this leads to distortions and errors in judgment. And each of us thinks: *The only real exception to this is* me. I *see things as they* really are. My *past experiences provide just me the insight and perspective to see them correctly. People who don't understand the world the way I do are either uninformed, or misguided, or willfully wrong.*[46]

We have parallel versions of the English language in secular and religious circles: the language of science and the language of the spiritual. How sad. Because in so many ways the languages have the same poetry, the same insight, only different words.

Vanity, vanity, all is vanity, says the Bible. We are all naive realists, says the psychology researcher. We all tacitly believe that our *own* experiences illuminate and make us wise, while for others their history explains their biases. The author of Ecclesiastes may be more elegant, but many modern ears understand the scientist better. It comes down to the same thing: don't take yourself too seriously.

If we can be open enough to see past our differences and translate the various metaphors we all use about God and goodness, we can avoid quite a lot of animosity. That's true for cultures as well as individuals.

Take one of the great debates in the United States today: evolution versus creationism. So many evolutionists viscerally dislike creationists and vice versa. I've drunk cocktails with enlightened rationalists in Washington, D.C., and heard that our problems can all be reduced to "those fundamentalists" down South; I've heard friends on their way to Bible study in the Carolinas shake their heads and despair about what "those liberals" up north are doing to the country.

In many ways I think that argument is about the nature of the sacred and the profane. For the good person in the Bible study group, it seems like a smug elite is determined to wring every bit of sacredness out of the fabric of our culture. The concept of evolution becomes redolent of the idea that there is no sacredness, that every iota of our world can be reduced to amoral, insensate dust. And that flies in the face of their experience—they have felt the power of goodness and faith in their lives.

On the other hand, the followers of liberal education have heard a lot about the follies of religion, have seen the narrow scope and fatal incompatibilities of many religions, have responded to the virtues of tolerance and open inquiry that seem anathema to many religions. And they are full of hope about the capabilities of science. To them, creationism is a rejection of the creative human effort to push back ignorance; it is intolerance and rigidity.

Notions of the sacred and the profane are ancient and, until our era, universal. Historians of religion have documented a notion of sacredness in all cultures. Going one step further, psychologist (and self-described atheist) Jonathan Haidt concludes from his research that the human mind perceives divinity and sacredness, whether or not God exists, and moreover that religious experiences are real and common (again, whether or not God exists).[47]

We all experience sacredness. Buddhist monks and Christian monks who undergo PET scans while they meditate and experience spiritual communion show activity in the same spot of their brains.[48] This sense of sacredness—the elevated feeling we have for people we love, for instance—is powerful for moving us to extraordinary action. Even if we are afraid of religion, afraid of the ways its power to move people can be misused, we'll lose something if we don't use this to help move ourselves to better action.

We have come to a point in history where we are all plot holders on a small island, an island with many rich and poor inhabitants, with no king and no unifying religion. We're nearsighted about our neighbors, but they are close enough to hurt us, or to resent us for our profligate ways. We've got no other place to go to. If we ignore the tightness of our neighborhood and fight and burn, we'll end up with a barren island (as archaeologists have shown did in fact happen on Easter Island centuries ago).

Frank

If we Americans don't act, our country and our world face a grim future. All sides in our American culture wars need to back down for the sake of our planet. Our political divisions paralyze us and render us incapable of working to fix what is broken in our human ecology.

God and Darwin Shake Hands

This means our ears have to be open to each other's concerns, even when it comes to our most iconic battles: pro-choice and pro-life, gay rights and traditional marriage, free trade and anti-globalism. Yes, that means that we can't all get what we want. Sometimes judges we don't like are going to be appointed; sometimes tax structures aren't going to be to the liking of all of us. Whichever party is in the majority must include the minority party in ways never seen before.

The Democrats alone can't save us. The Republicans alone can't save us. The religious community alone can't save us. The secular community alone can't save us. Liberals or conservatives alone can't save us. We can't behave any longer as if this country is a series of embittered church splits. We have to stop treating each other as heretics.

What is life about? It's *not* about "winning." Abandoned on a desert island, we'll all make the same choices. The feminist mother or fundamentalist father, the atheist or the believer, will almost always put their children's good ahead of themselves.

17. A Marriage of Equals

★ ════════════════════════

Frank

There is an essential thing we call human nature that unites us. God is love, the Bible tells us. And whether we believe that or not, we all know, deep down, that life *is* about love; for our children, our grandchildren, our planet, and all those we will never meet, those who one day will share that thrill of recognition as they connect with other human beings and our beautiful earth.

It will be that love that will make us back away from the hate we have fallen into. Those who divide us must be seen for what they are: a threat to human survival. Yes, that means that in the American context it must become as unacceptable to try to win by politics as usual as it would be to try to win by stripping black men and women of the vote, something unthinkable today.

We are past the time that we can simply delegate "figuring things out" to someone else, as though government is something separate from us. We're past the point that we can feel satisfaction with merely "expressing our opinions" about things to like-minded people and feel like we've accomplished anything. It's time to demand that our system change, because it has to in order to lead a robust and talented population to feel less alienated and dissatisfied.

Americans used to be the freest people in the world. Not anymore. We may have more influence over our personal consumer choices than ever before, but not over our government. We are treated as consumer suckers, playthings of advertisers, conditioned to crave what we don't need and can't afford.

Each year the barriers to being part of the decisions that shape our country and world grow. You need more and more money to run for office. A smaller and smaller self-perpetuating elite of specialists dominates politics. And our military is a "professional" fighting force, no longer made up of citizen-soldiers in a cross-cultural, cross-class shared melting-pot experience. We are a more class-ridden society than ever.

What does "we" mean in America today? Not much more than cohabiting, at the moment. Instead it could be—must become—a marriage.

A Marriage of Equals

Kathy

Can we Americans find a commitment, a transcendent purpose great enough to keep us together in tough times? Can we
forge a more perfect union for the challenges ahead?

Frank

Marriage, at its best, requires goodwill, patience, cooperation,
forgiveness, gratitude, respect, and the ability to not take yourself too seriously. Self-involved people are unhappy people, and
the unlucky sods they're married to are in even worse shape.
That's what we Americans are: a nation of self-involved piss-
ers and moaners blaming everyone but ourselves.

Mea culpa! Shame on us. Shame on me.

Want to change? In my case, loving Genie helped. The needs
of my children helped. Fear of God helped. And it also helps
to have a sense of commitment to the long haul, and faith that
you're in this boat with the right person. It helps to have a belief
in an ultimate purpose. That is what gets a married couple over
their differences: a greater cause. Children, for instance.

Kathy

I met my husband when I was thirty, married at thirty-three.
Before that, I had pretty much just mastered being Kathy. I

had plenty of time for trial and error and mental note taking. I figured out my likes and dislikes, strengths and weaknesses, broad-brush goals and values, so when it came time for life decisions, I felt pretty confident deciding what was best for me.

Then suddenly, after I got married, that locus of decision making shifted. It wasn't inside me, and it wasn't inside Greg; it was someplace in the middle. From that point on, Greg and I both made decisions that we wouldn't have made by ourselves—his decision to do an extra year of graduate study, my decision to go to Okinawa to be with him on that Marine base—but each of those seemed like the right decision for Greg and Kathy. And over time those decisions changed again when we grew to Greg and Kathy and Sophie, and eventually to Greg and Kathy and Sophie and Charley.

There are two models of marriage. In one, the individual essentially stays the same, and the spouse is good as long as he or she make things better (or at least not worse) for the individual. In the second model, the individual remains, but also changes deeply.

Frank

I took the opposite road and got married as a teen. Genie and I finished growing up together. And yet years later Kathy and I both understand married life in a similar way. We are both in marriages that work because we understand that we're part of something, not the thing all by ourselves. Change the names to Frank and Genie and Jessica and Francis and John (and add in my wonderful son-in-law, Dani, and lovely daughter-in-law, Becky, and my grandchildren, Amanda and Benjamin) and the Schaeffer family tells the same story of transformation.

So what does taking another look at our national "marriage" mean? We need to prepare our children to grow up and become part of a national family, contributing to it and making it better with their character and talents, and changed by those with whom they share the family home—our nation. That means starting with education.

Love and work make life meaningful, said Freud. Character and connection are the recipe for a good life, Kathy tells me the positivist psychologists say. Redemption through facing adversity is taught by all religions. It's time we reeducate ourselves (and our children) as to the real meaning of life.

Kathy

America invented the idea of free education because we needed people who could read and write, reason, and have character to operate the new country. But education was understood as a type of soul food. It wasn't only about producing productive workers; it was also about helping students become ethical and complete human beings with a strong moral compass, who could be capable of running a country. We still need to train ourselves in character skills as much as those for work, and it's training we can all use at every stage of our lives.

Social scientists lead by the University of Pennsylvania have distilled six character traits consistent across cultures, geography, and time; they are wisdom and knowledge, courage, humanity, justice, temperance, and transcendence. We need to find those characteristics in ourselves and our children and cultivate their development. And we cultivate not just by learning, but by doing too—by being loyal, not just thinking about loyalty, for instance.

Frank

The idea that human beings live by more than bread alone, that character is formed and taught through an appreciation of transcendent themes, has been visited and revisited by artists and writers, composers and philosophers through the ages. These days it's possible to grow up and live, ignoring the ethical and moral lessons of the ages. We as a culture have absorbed the "lesson" of striving for a consumer society stripped of transcendent purpose or themes. It has given way to standardized tests on the most rudimentary of a diminishing number of subjects. And since we are one of the first societies ever to try to strip moral instruction out of education, the spiritual context for the most basic subjects is missing.

In a postmodern educational system designed to produce consumers and determined to avoid "moralizing," one can study Isaac Newton's science but never know about his evangelical theological writings. So the student might get the science but never the philosophy that made it seem worthwhile to Newton: the idea of an orderly creation created by a reasonable and personal God. And how may Shakespeare's *Macbeth* or a movie like *Blade Runner* be understood without knowl-edge of the inherently religious moral/philosophical (and spe-cifically biblical) narratives whence they are derived?

The goal of education should be not only to create people literate in rudimentary reading, math, and science, people who can "earn a living" as grown-ups, or "compete in the global marketplace," but also to build the skills that let people participate in and change our society and enjoy the fullness of our lovely world. Without that sense of joy, why would they bother to participate or make the sacrifices needed to save our beleaguered democracy and earth?

But talking about education without addressing spiritual health, or the lack of it, when it comes to our families is futile. We need to begin with our families and stop lying to our-selves. Divorce hurts no matter how "well" or "sensitively" it's done. A happy family requires sacrifices, sometimes big ones, of time, career, material things. We need to stop being suckered into abandoning our children to TV as a babysitter, to that iPod, computer, and text messaging that are eating into time with children. We are entertainment addicts!

A generation of Americans risk betraying their children and themselves. We know it. We feel guilty. We should. But there is a way back. It's called repentance. That road is open to both religious and secular people. Kathy is right: you don't have to believe in God to change your life. But you *do* have to admit that we've been listening to (and filling our lives with) bullshit.

That change can begin with families staying together and sacrificing for each other, even when it hurts to do so. Yes, that means we'll miss out on some things. Not everything is win-win. Some things are right, period.

The change can include less dramatic acts such as going to that "boring" local town meeting and discovering that getting to know our actual physical neighbors isn't boring after all. Maybe by working with them we can put in sidewalks and make our towns more human-friendly. Maybe we can find a way to take all the kids in the sixth grade to a play. Maybe that marriage in the house two doors down from you is breaking up because a young mother or a middle-aged husband feels isolated and unsupported. Maybe you'll meet that person at the meeting and invite him or her over.

And this from the "God guy": how stupid to allow churches to have a corner on the market of community! There are other ways to come together that have good results—for instance, those town meetings that get the sidewalks put in and restore the arts to the school curriculum and help a young mom make friends. That is also true spirituality, "for faith without works is dead."

Then there is the need to seriously reform the national curriculum. We had founding fathers who had great, if imperfectly applied, ideas. There is no harm in venerating them, even when we portray them as fully human—and, in some cases, as egregious sinners who held slaves.

First things first. Young Americans need to know that they are very lucky people. They also need to know that luck won't maintain what they have. It will take their participation. So the first lesson for the American young person must be about what it means to be an American, someone standing on the shoulders of giants—like Madison, Jefferson, and Locke—who gave us the unique ideas that made it possible to govern ourselves freely.

Civics should also include unashamedly teaching patriotism and the symbols of American democracy, and encouraging (perhaps requiring) all students to serve—in the military or in a civilian capacity—as a way to become part of our melting pot, not to mention as a vital part of growing up.

Kathy and I hope that after intense and serious study of civics is reintroduced in all grades, we will embrace a nationwide curriculum that imparts a full vision of what life can be. Classical music and jazz, art and art history, fiction writing, languages, theater, nature studies, and outdoor projects should be treated as the real basics and absolute essentials, not "extras." They are those things that spark creativity and spirituality, that make life sweet and good. Without them our educational system is doing nothing more than producing drones, more worthy of Huxley's *Brave New World* dystopia than of the vision of our founders.

Kathy

It's not only our kids we'll need to train, it's ourselves. All evidence says that the last Greatest Generation was so great because they were trained. They learned how to engage. It became a habit for them. We need to teach ourselves the same habits. And some of these changes have to happen to society through changes in laws.

Doing *is* learning. Organizations in which people practice developing ideas and arguing and compromising and mobilizing are tremendously useful to civic society. Yes, that includes churches, temples, and mosques. It also includes many other types of gatherings.

Membership organizations really are good for people and society. Let's privilege them, encourage them by giving better tax breaks to nonprofits that have actual members, rather than elaborate professional lobbying programs. Let's get people into the habit of engaging with national service too. It needn't be an enormous government bureaucracy. We can simply encourage a gap year between high school and college, where people stay at home or make other private arrangements and volunteer for a qualified nonprofit, and award loans or grants accordingly.

But we have to not only train people but also be willing to deliver the goods to people. We have to be willing to put more of the reins into the hands of we the people.

In Switzerland there's a lot of direct democracy. Denmark practices this too. So perhaps it's no coincidence that both also rate at the top in polls of individuals' trust in their government.

The time has come to trust the American people enough to try direct democracy here. In the age of the Internet we could make this very possible. We should consider ideas like a right of petition that can force a revote on an issue. Frank and I like that idea even if something we dislike gets voted in. We both believe that there is something far more fatal to our democracy than losing on this or that issue: a sense of being disconnected from one's own fate. We think that the process is sometimes as important as, or more important than, the outcome. We need to find ways to make our democracy include us all again and give us a sense of ownership.

Frank

We've got to change the way people's behavior has been shaped by peer pressure. When the drivers of gas guzzlers encounter a wall of furious disdain, we'll see fewer SUVs, giant pickups, and big cars on the road. We might also see proper levels of funding for trains, better-developed high-density communities where commuting isn't needed, fewer corporate jets in the air, and more people walking. When educators, parents, and entertainers understand that they will face the just fury of a nation if they do not begin to teach values, civics, the arts, and patriotism—and manners based on non-negotiable morals—there will be changes. When the social pressure is on mothers and fathers to make sacrifices and do the work to stay together for the good of their children, we'll see fewer divorces and thus less terrible dislocation in children's lives, not to mention a drastic reduction in economic hardship. When it's no longer considered cool to meet every contingency with an ironic sneer, who knows—sincerity might even make a comeback and not be dismissed out of hand as retrograde earnestness.

The argument for our nation's renewed civic life, as well as the argument for the defense of our earth against destruction, has to be cast in terms of morality and taboos. If facts alone worked, the no-fault divorce laws in every state would have been rethought just on the basis of their economic impact. No child would even see a TV before the age of three and would never watch more than an hour a day thereafter. We'd all be driving electric cars, and we would have spent the money Bush wasted in Iraq on a crash program of alternative energy development.

We have the facts. What we don't have is the moral will. There has to be some element that deals in the currency of right and wrong, the equivalent of my son John wanting to light all those candles in our Greek Orthodox church as a way of coming to terms with his wartime experiences.

Any hope of changing Americans' behavior without an appeal to basic morality will fail. That is because we are who we are as human beings, for better or worse. And Americans' religious and ethical history makes us even more susceptible to moral and religious arguments.

Let's harness that energy. The resonance of the language of religion, values, meaning, and purpose is too powerful to consign to locked cupboards. If we want to move mountains, we need to be unafraid of words like *grace, redemption, holy*, and *calling*.

18. Blending Voices

Frank and Kathy—Kathy and Frank

When Kathy got married, a coworker offered her a piece of advice: "Remember," he said, "no opinion you have is more important than the relationship." It's one of the best bits of advice either of us has heard.

If winning is everything, then you won't want participation: it might derail your plans. But if participation *is* winning, because it strengthens democracy, then figuring out the fastest way to win every issue (by running to the courts, or redrawing the map of congressional districts, or cleverly outspending your opponent—whatever) can be losing.

So many voices are calling for change now. Here we argue

that this change requires us to rethink the American Dream and our obligations. For many of us, the strongest impetus for change will be the imperative to act to save the earth from climate change. But we can't do that unless we first face the fact that we've created a society that specializes in trivializing the human condition. If life in America remains about consuming, about "I want," about always "winning" politically, we're lost.[49]

Character matters. Who we train ourselves to be matters. But we seem to be working hard to strip character—the moral fortitude to do hard things—out of our souls. Something needs to jog us awake. We can laugh or bury our heads in the sand, but the truth is that laissez-faire people aren't going to do good things for our earth, for our country, or, ultimately, for themselves.

We need a secular version of conversion that both religious and secular people can sign on to. Creating and contributing to that effort can have wide-reaching effects. It can rejuvenate the family, education, participation, social ecology, earthly ecology, human ecology.

According to geologist Jared Diamond, there is a model for success that has worked before. Numerous self-contained small-scale rural societies that have managed their own resources well, from the Pueblo Indians of North America to the alpine Swiss villages, have lasted many hundreds of years and sometimes longer because they were in balance with their local environment.

Diamond points out that our earth is experiencing the same kind of drastic and obvious depletion of resources and degradation of the environment worldwide that discrete societies have experienced in the past on a more local level and dealt with by choice. He suggests that if we learn the lessons of the societies that have grappled with this before, we can find our way to surviving our current crisis. We think this model of resource management is a good model for larger societal change.

His solution requires the change that we are advocating. According to Diamond, the solution most likely to work is to have individuals—citizens—recognize their common interests and design, obey, and enforce a solution themselves.[50] According to Diamond, this requires four conditions to work. To paraphrase:

1. That we the people recognize ourselves as a natural group.
2. That we trust and communicate with each other.
3. That we expect to share a common future and pass our resources on to our heirs.
4. That we are capable of organizing and policing ourselves, and permitted to do so.

The American politics of today needs to be tuned toward creating these four conditions. Because we need our government's actions to be *our* actions, we need to embrace shared identity and be willing to see ourselves as Americans in a shared endeavor.

This is one reason that a renewed civics curriculum and commitment to the arts and humanities in all grades are so important, since they foster a cultural identity we can share. It is time to reclaim a celebration of the American idea. We can and should make the concept of "being American" mean "being our better selves." America's cultural identity is not about consuming more than other people, or working longer hours, or other bare facts.

What is a cultural identity we can all share? It's rooted in the values of Western civilization with a magnificent humanizing twist. All free men and women belong to us—all ideas that expound on the essential dignity of humankind are ours, even if they come from overseas. This is not chauvinism: other countries can be equally dynamic and have their own narratives to craft, and ultimately all nations and people can contribute to the world. But because of our history and because humans are still grouped in nations, we have something distinct to contribute as Americans. America's cultural identity is her aspirational identity: what she can be at her best, what can make us better by association.

The eras have changed. Consumerism and self-expression, though they may have been useful at one time, have outlived their usefulness. As the town criers called when an old era ended and a new one began, "The King is dead, long live the King." So what's next?

A New National Purpose

The "marriage" of three hundred million people needs a renewed and transcendent purpose to replace the simple consumerism and simple self-expression that have led to terminally self-destructive selfishness. That purpose is *being American*.

What does "being American" mean? It is not some new form of jingoistic nationalism. It is not a state-sponsored replacement for a moral or religious vision of life. It is not "all about me," and it is not all about "what I think or feel." It is not about being defined by our differences—not about being heterosexual, evangelical, gay, Jewish, Roman Catholic, Orthodox, Protestant, Hindu, Muslim, anti-gay, pro-life, pro-choice, feminist, atheist, fundamentalist, Democratic, or Republican. It is not about identity politics.

Being American *is* about our common obligations to each other and to our planet—the obligations that people on lifeboats have to one another. It is about freeing ourselves from the myths, lies, and false metaphors—"Consume!" "Express!" "Choose!" "Spend!"—that are eating away at our ability to function as a society in every area of life. It is about rediscovering life understood as a transcendent experience, where altruism makes sense again, because individual and collective acts of service (mitzvahs) turn us into better people. It is about recognizing that we have a common bond with everyone we meet on this earth, because America is not an island—it is just another human community on our island-sized, shrinking planet.

The enemy is not the "other" but our actual situation, for which we all bear responsibility. Our collective degradation of the earth's ability to sustain life is one of the mountains we need to move. The soundness of our next generation—of America—is everyone's business.

Being American means something particular. It means more than living inside a set of borders or sharing a family name, ethnic background, skin color, or religion. We are the country that taught the world that millions of otherwise unconnected people can run their own show and build something dynamic, something that's even (sometimes) a force for good. We did this not on the basis of blood ties, tribe, or any one religion. We did this based on good ideas—the best ideas that any human society has ever been founded on.

Our American inheritance, as expressed in our Declaration of Independence and Constitution, is the most compelling set of political first principles ever written. That is the contract with the future we have signed on to just by living here. We have to bring this language of inspiration—language that includes being endowed by our Creator with inalienable rights—back into the public space without fear of what some people might think or say.

We have to choose to do this. It won't happen by itself. It *isn't* happening by itself. We don't all have to agree, just as we here—Frank and Kathy—don't agree about everything. But we like and respect each other. And we know we are in the same boat, a boat neither of us can navigate alone. Agree or not, we need each other.

Acting to Save the Future

We can no longer afford the hate speech that passes for political discourse, from either the right or the left. And we can't afford to hand our fate over to an interchangeable coterie of "professionals" and multimillionaires in both political parties. We need to act.

As part of boot camp training, a group of recruits is given a task—say, to get to the other side of a swift muddy river, or to build a tower—with no tools or obvious materials. The recruits have to figure out how to work together to come up with ideas, make decisions, and execute them. The real goal isn't to build the tower. It's to find out whether this group of people can work out a problem, put themselves in a kind of order that allows them to get things done, work as a team. This lesson applied to our national situation should involve:

- Thinking about the ideals and values you most believe in for you and your family. Writing them down as something you stand for. Seeing how you can live those ideals and teaching them to your children as part of your daily life. Asking yourself what you can change in order to live those ideals more than you do today. If you feel trapped, perhaps you can untrap yourself. If you agree with us that our culture needs to change, what are you doing to buck the trend in order to become countercultural?

- Civic education in school and beyond should be about learning and reclaiming the American ideals that bind us together and give us a basis for being our better selves, so that patriotism is both about creating a national family and about aspiring for more. The American ideals we celebrate here are ideas of the intrinsic worth of all individuals, because all men and women are created equal. Notions of freedom and fairness need to extend beyond "what's in it for me." Soul education is about creating people of character who can help craft a more humane future, not only pass tests and contribute to consumer confidence.

- We need to act and train ourselves constantly to engage with one another to collaborate, compromise, contribute, whether it is through the PTA or the Rotary Club, the Sierra Club or groups we start, or through national service or military service.

- We need new forms of direct democracy. If the government wants engaged citizens, it needs to hand over some of the reins. Let's ask Americans to be accountable for our opinions and accept the responsibility for steering the country and use new technology. Unless we accept a country by, for, and of lobbyists, we have no alternative but to make it by, for, and of *us*.

The necessity for individuals to transcend our narrow selves isn't optional, no matter how delusional we are or how pointless life is. If God has a wonderful plan for us, it is not to destroy our planet's ability to support human life. If God doesn't exist, survival is still the issue.

We are graced to be living in a time where a momentous purpose is thrust upon us. Our earth is in deep trouble. Our democracy is weakening. The mountains we need to move are bigger than anything we have faced before. We are the generation that will answer two questions through our action or inaction: Can the notion that power belongs to the people survive? Can we husband what we have on this earth so future generations can flourish?

Act for the pleasure of it, act for anticipation of future glory, act for our children.

Notes

1. There are shelves of books and studies on these topics. Some good ones are *The Loss of Happiness in Market Economies* by Robert E. Lane, a Yale political scientist, which gives a political and economic perspective; *Happiness* by Richard Layard, a well-known British economist; *Authentic Happiness*, by Martin Seligman, Ph.D., the founder of the Positive psychology movement; *The Happiness Hypothesis* by psychology professor Jonathan Haidt; and *The High Price of Materialism* by psychologist Tim Kasser. The Dalai Lama wrote a wonderful book on the subject, *The Art of Happiness*, coauthored with psychoanalyst Howard Cutler, M.D., from the Buddhist perspective. Many of these books share similar research and studies, which all reinforce the argument that money doesn't buy happiness.

Notes

2. Matthew 7:27.

3. For instance, Robert Lane cites research that shows
    that most people believe life would be better with a 25
    percent pay increase—but those at the higher level are
    not, in fact, happier with their lives. *Loss of Happiness*, p. 71.
    Moreover, materialism—valuing material things
    more than the nonmaterial (believing that money
    and stuff will make you happy) seems to have a negative
    effect on your actual happiness. Materialists, in other
    words, rate themselves as less happy than less materialistic
    people. According to psychology researcher Martin
    Seligman, people who value money at all levels of real
    income more than other goals are less satisfied with their
    income and lives as a whole. *Authentic Happiness*, p. 55.

4. *The Autobiography of Charles Darwin, 1809–1882,* ed.
    Nora Barlow (New York: W. W. Norton, 1993), p. 93.

5. Lee M. Silver, *Challenging Nature: The Clash of Science and
    Spirituality at the New Frontier of Life* (New York: Ecco,
    2006), p. 214.

6. Manifest Destiny followed from the idea that America
    was exceptional and it was part of God's purpose that its
    virtues of republican democracy should spread. The
    founders, especially Thomas Jefferson, Benjamin Franklin,
    and George Mason, wrote extensively on this subject,
    though the phrase "Manifest Destiny" itself wasn't coined
    until the mideighteenth century, by journalist John
    O'Sullivan. In our first era, this is how people's individual
    dreams of the good life twinned with the national purpose
    of expansion. An excellent modern discussion of this

idea can be found in Michael Sandel's *Democracy's Discontent*. The pioneers and settlers and cattlemen were pursuing their personal dreams of personal success *and* America's idea of its greater purpose at the same time and with powerful results. It is true Manifest Destiny hurt a lot of Native Americans. But America would not have been America without that expansion.

7. Harvard sociologist Theda Skocpol recently wrote a book elaborating and proving this point: *Diminished Democracy: From Membership to Management in American Civil Life* (Norman: University of Oklahoma Press, 2004).

8. Poll by Lake Research Partners released September 2006. Available online at www.changetowin.org/features/the-american-dream-survey.html.

9. Camille Sweeney, "The Middle of the Middle Class," *New York Times Magazine,* June 9, 2002, cited in Gregg Easterbrook, *The Progress Paradox* (New York: Random House, 2003), p. 15. If you count supermarket-prepared meals, many people are freed from actually making their own food. The average work week was six 11-hour days in 1900; now it's about five 8-hour days on average.

10. Bruno S. Frey and Alois Stutzer, *Happiness and Economics: How the Economy and Institutions Affect Human Well-Being* (Princeton University Press, 2002), p. 76.

11. Easterbrook, *The Progress Paradox*, p. 164.

12. David Myers, *The American Paradox: Spiritual Hunger in the Age of Plenty* (New Haven: Yale University Press, 2001), p. 5.

13. Robert Lane, *The Loss of Happiness in Market Democracies* (New Haven: Yale University Press, 2000), p. 85.

Notes

14. Ibid., p. 27.

15. Pew poll reported December 2007.

16. Robert Samuelson, *The Good Life and Its Discontents* (New York: Random House, 1995).

17. These surveys are discussed in several books that examine the conundrum American families face. Two are *The Two-Income Trap* by Elizabeth Warren and Amelia Warren Tyagi (New York: Basic Books, 2003) and the *Overspent American* by Juliet Schorr (New York: HarperPerrenial, 1998). In the *Two-Income Trap*, the authors, who are economists, explain how two incomes now buy what one income used to (a house in a safe neighborhood with good schools and the appliances and amenities that neighbors also have).

18. Study by Brown and Harris, *The Social Origins of Depression*, (New York: The Free Press, 1978), p. 103, cited in Lane, *Loss of Happiness*, p. 85.

19. Lane, *Loss of Happiness*, pp. 28–29.

20. Schorr, *Overspent American*, p. 165.

21. Pew Research Center poll reported in "A Qualified Yes to Global Trade," *International Herald Tribune,* October 5, 2007.

22. Christopher Key Chapple, "Hinduism, Jainism, and Ecology" (2004), Forum on Religion and Ecology, Harvard University Center for the Environment, available at http://environment.harvard.edu/religion/religion/hinduism/index.html.

23. Daniel B. Fink, "Judaism and Ecology: A Theology of Creation," *Earth Ethics* 10, 1 (1998), available at

http://environment.harvard.edu/religion/religion/
judaism/index.html.

24. Karen Armstrong, *The Great Transformation: The
Beginning of Our Religious Traditions* (Knopf, 2006).

25. David Lilienthal, first director of Roosevelt's Tennessee
Valley Authority.

26. British sociologist Anthony Giddins has written
extensively about the idea of Modernity as a distinct
sociological period, and identifies it, among other
things, as being associated with industrialization and
the rise of the nation-state. But the basis of our economy
is no longer industrialization. And the ordering of our
international relations is no longer around the
consolidation of the nation-state. It is more and more
about nations organizing and interacting with each other
(such as the European Union and other increasingly
influential regional unions).

27. Andrew Higgins, "Split over Global Warming Widens
Among Evangelicals," *Wall Street Journal*, September 28,
2007.

28. Economists Frey and Stutzer's book, *Happiness and
Economics*, looks at worldwide indices of happiness as
well as controls for a number of factors. The authors find
that the kind of society you live in affects your happiness.
And that the more participatory your society, the happier
you will be, all else being equal. The Swiss, as it happens,
are among the countries that allow for the most direct
participation by their citizens.

29. These findings are echoed in Seligman, *Authentic Happiness*,

pp. 55–61; Lane, *Loss of Happiness*, p. 327; Frey and Stutzer, *Happiness and Economics*, p. 174; Robert Putnam, *Bowling Alone* (New York: Simon and Schuster, 2000), p. 288; and no doubt many others.

30.   Putnam connects the dots on social activity, personal well-being, and social good. As he concludes: "People who have active and trusting connections to others—whether family members, friends, or fellow bowlers—develop or maintain character traits that are good for the rest of society. Joiners become more tolerant, less cynical, and more empathetic to the misfortunes of others." (*Bowling Alone*, p. 288).

31.   The study, by University of Michigan researcher James House, is described in Dalai Lama and Howard Cutler, *The Art of Happiness* (New York: Riverhead Books, 1998), p. 126.

32.   Jonathan Haidt, *The Happiness Hypothesis: Finding Modern Truth in Ancient Wisdom* (New York: Basic Books, 2006), p. 174.

33.   Study by George Vallant, quoted in Haidt, p. 126.

34.   This is a study Haidt himself conducted with his classes, and it is described in the *Happiness Hypothesis*, pp. 97–98.

35.   For instance, Google's initial public offering made this philosophy clear by spelling out to potential shareholders that the company did not plan to focus on short-term profits. See "Letter to Shareholders," available at http://investor.google.com/ipo_letter.html.

36.   Lord James Bryce, *The American Commonwealth* (New York: Macmillan, 1895), 2:278, quoted in Theda Skocpol,

Notes

Diminished Democracy: From Membership to Management in American Civil Life (Norman: University of Oklahoma Press, 2004), p. 22. How did they do this? Based on exhaustive research covering hundreds of groups, Skocpol describes scenes of meetings where members would gather, take notes, and learn rules of order and the sharing of responsibility. They would sponsor debates on two sides of a current issue—the point wasn't to have made up your mind before you participated, but to actually become educated through your participation. For example, the meeting programs for the (women's) Progressive Study Club in Henry, South Dakota, in 1916 included discussions of music and travel some weeks, and expositions on subjects such as immigration and national defenses (*Diminished Democracy*, p. 120).

37. Skocpol, *Diminished Democracy*, p. 161.
38. Ibid., pp. 183–85; quote on p. 185.
39. Robert D. Putnam, *Bowling Alone: The Collapse and Revival of American Community* (New York: Simon and Schuster, 2000), p. 185.
40. Dr. David Myers, an award-winning researcher and educator whose most recent is *The American Paradox: Spiritual Hunger in an Age of Plenty* (New Haven: Yale University Press, 2000).
41. Seligman, *Authentic Happiness*, pp. 59–60.
42. Robert Wright, *The Moral Animal* (New York: Pantheon, 1994), pp. 324–35; quote on p. 325.
43. Francis Schaeffer and Udo Middelmann, *Pollution and the Death of Man* (Wheaton, IL: Tyndale House, 1970), p. 128.

44. Myers, *The American Paradox*, pp. 294–95.

45. Richard Dawkins, *The Selfish Gene,* 2nd ed. (New York: Oxford University Press, 1989), pp. 67, 84.

46. The psychologists who discovered and demonstrated naive realism are Lee Pronin of Princeton and Lee Ross of Stanford. They uncovered this as they were studying the difficulty of negotiating settlements in lawsuits even when the proposed settlement leads to more money for the litigants than a lawsuit does, when a great deal of money goes to the lawyers. In other words, people aren't rational actors.

47. Haidt makes a psychological statement but also points out that the same argument has been made by historians. He cites the *Sacred and the Profane* by Mircea Eliade, a noted religion historian, which also demonstrates the universality of humanity's ability to perceive sacredness. (San Diego, CA: Harcourt Brace, 1959). Jonathan Haidt, *The Happiness Hypothesis* (New York: Basic Books, 2006), pp. 184, 192.

48. A large number of studies are discussed in a book by cellular geneticist-turned-Buddhist monk, Matthieu Ricard, in his chapter on "Happiness in the Lab." Two landmark studies are "Long-Term Meditators Self-Induce High Amplitude Gamma Synchrony During Mental Practice, PNAS 101:46 (Nov. 16, 2004); and "Alterations in Brain and Immune Fuction Produced by Mindfulness Meditation," *Psychosomatic Medicine* 65 (2003), pp. 564–70. Matthieu Ricard, *Happiness: A Guide to Developing Life's*

Most Important Skill (London: Atlantic Books, 2007),
pp. 186–201.

49.   Of course, politically, Senator Obama has made change
the center of his platform. He's called for an end to
divisiveness too. In the social sciences, many otherwise
staid scholars have called for change. Environmentalists
point out change is necessary or we may destroy
ourselves. Jared Diamond argues that we are sitting atop
a time bomb with a fuse of fifty years at best. Further,
he adds, we have the technology to solve our problems;
we just lack the political will to apply solutions already
available. *Collapse*, p. 522.

Robert Lane argues that the problem before us "is to
transcend the market culture. . . . Like all major
transitions, the proposed transition will be painful,
although, like the transition from agriculture to
industrial society . . . [it] has a shared value: well-being in
this world." *Loss of Happiness*, p. 328. Lane says,
"Americans are right that the bonds of our communities
have withered, and we are right to fear that this
transformation has very real costs. The challenge for us,
however, as it was for our predecessors moving from the
Gilded Age to the Progressive Era, is not to grieve over
social change, but to guide it." *Bowling Alone*, p. 402.

50.   Jared Diamond, *Collapse: How Societies Choose to Fail or
Succeed* (New York: Penguin, 2005), p. 429.